WHY ME?

A Comedy

by Stanley Price

Copyright © 1986 by Zophar Limited
All Rights Reserved

WHY ME? is fully protected under the copyright laws of the British Commonwealth, including Canada, the United States of America, and all other countries of the Copyright Union. All rights, including professional and amateur stage productions, recitation, lecturing, public reading, motion picture, radio broadcasting, television, online/digital production, and the rights of translation into foreign languages are strictly reserved.

ISBN 978-0-573-01622-6

concordtheatricals.co.uk
concordtheatricals.com

FOR PRODUCTION ENQUIRIES
UNITED KINGDOM AND WORLD
EXCLUDING NORTH AMERICA
licensing@concordtheatricals.co.uk
020-7054-7298

NORTH AMERICA
info@concordtheatricals.com
1-866-979-0447

Each title is subject to availability from Concord Theatricals, depending upon country of performance.

CAUTION: Professional and amateur producers are hereby warned that *WHY ME?* is subject to a licensing fee. The purchase, renting, lending or use of this book does not constitute a licence to perform this title(s), which licence must be obtained from the appropriate agent prior to any performance. Performance of this title(s) without a licence is a violation of copyright law and may subject the producer and/or presenter of such performances to penalties. Both amateurs and professionals considering a production are strongly advised to apply to the appropriate agent before starting rehearsals, advertising, or booking a theatre. A licensing fee must be paid whether the title is presented for charity or gain and whether or not admission is charged.

This work is published by Samuel French, an imprint of Concord Theatricals Ltd.

Professional rights in this title are controlled by Concord Theatricals, Aldwych House, 71-91 Aldwych, London, WC2B 4HN

No one shall make any changes in this title for the purpose of production. No part of this book may be reproduced, stored in a retrieval system, scanned, uploaded, or transmitted in any form, by any means, now known or yet to be invented, including mechanical, electronic, digital, photocopying, recording, videotaping, or otherwise, without the prior written permission of the publisher. No one shall share this title, or part of this title, to any social media or file hosting websites.

The moral right of Stanley Price to be identified as author of this work has been asserted in accordance with Section 77 of the Copyright, Designs and Patents Act 1988.

USE OF COPYRIGHTED MUSIC

A licence issued by Concord Theatricals to perform this play does not include permission to use the incidental music specified in this publication. In the United Kingdom: Where the place of performance is already licensed by the PERFORMING RIGHT SOCIETY (PRS) a return of the music used must be made to them. If the place of performance is not so licensed then application should be made to PRS for Music (www.prsformusic.com). A separate and additional licence from PHONOGRAPHIC PERFORMANCE LTD (www.ppluk.com) may be needed whenever commercial recordings are used. Outside the United Kingdom: Please contact the appropriate music licensing authority in your territory for the rights to any incidental music.

USE OF COPYRIGHTED THIRD-PARTY MATERIALS

Licensees are solely responsible for obtaining formal written permission from copyright owners to use copyrighted third-party materials (e.g., artworks, logos) in the performance of this play and are strongly cautioned to do so. If no such permission is obtained by the licensee, then the licensee must use only original materials that the licensee owns and controls. Licensees are solely responsible and liable for clearances of all third-party copyrighted materials, and shall indemnify the copyright owners of the play(s) and their licensing agent, Concord Theatricals Ltd., against any costs, expenses, losses and liabilities arising from the use of such copyrighted third-party materials by licensees.

IMPORTANT BILLING AND CREDIT REQUIREMENTS

If you have obtained performance rights to this title, please refer to your licensing agreement for important billing and credit requirements.

CHARACTERS

John Bailey
Helen Bailey, his wife
Mary Ferguson, her mother
Arthur Hollis, a neighbour
Gwen Hollis, his wife
Tom Bailey, the Baileys' son

The action is set in the Baileys' South London house over a long summer

ACT I   Scene 1 Early evening
        Scene 2 Some weeks later. Morning
        Scene 3 Some days later. Morning
        Scene 4 A few days later. Early evening

ACT II Scene 1 A few weeks later. Morning
        Scene 2 That night
        Scene 3 The next morning
        Scene 4 A couple of weeks later. Afternoon

Time—the present

WHY ME?

First presented in London at the Strand Theatre on 5th March, 1985, with the following cast of characters:

John Bailey	Richard Briers
Mary Ferguson	Liz Smith
Helen Bailey	Diane Fletcher
Gwen Hollis	Polly Hemingway
Arthur Hollis	Eamon Boland
Tom Bailey	Ian Targett

Directed by Robert Chetwyn
Designed by Joe Vanek

ACT I

Scene 1

The living-room of the Baileys' house in South London. Summer. Early evening

The living-room is a double area, knocked through on the ground floor of a smallish Victorian villa in a South London suburb like Greenwich or Blackheath. The living-area spills across both parts of the room, which now consists of a living and dining-area. The Baileys have lived in the house for two years and have clearly not had the time, or the money, to finish the interior of the room properly or coherently. The room thus lacks a certain unity, and the two original Victorian fireplaces are still in each section of the room (one has to be in the invisible fourth wall). The Baileys previously lived in a modern house and brought some of their contemporary furniture with them. A few Victorian pieces have recently been added. In the living-area the sofa, armchair and coffee table are modern, two other easy-chairs are Victorian. Along the UR *wall is a modern shelving cupboard unit with books and a hi-fi set. Besides the books are some family photographs and some professional magazines and files. Beside this is a Victorian glass-fronted cabinet that contains glasses and drink. At the* L *end of the double-room is a modern dining-table pushed against a wall and four Victorian dining-chairs.* C *is a desk with a phone. A door from the dining-area leads into a small kitchen. The door from the living-room leads into the hall. The house is double-fronted so that, visible on the other side of the hall, is another door exactly opposite the living-room door. This leads to Mary Ferguson's granny-flat*

The Errol Garner recording of "Summertime" plays. When the CURTAIN *rises there is the sound of the front door opening and shutting, as quietly as possible*

After a moment John Bailey comes into the living-room. He wears a well-cut, dark grey suit, a blue shirt, and a subdued patterned tie. He carries a briefcase, and looks every inch a successful professional man who has had a hard day at the office. He comes into the room, treading softly as though to avoid disturbing anybody else in the house. He shuts the door quietly behind him. He puts his briefcase down on the desk, sits down, and his shoulders slump. For a moment, he looks whacked, and then anger takes over. He bangs his fist down on the briefcase. Angry and frustrated, he takes a file from his briefcase and hurls it on to the floor. He takes a couple of deep breaths, trying to control himself. He takes his jacket off, throws it on a chair, and crosses to the Victorian cabinet that contains the drink. He gets out a glass and a bottle of whisky. The bottle is empty. He puts it back and gets out a fancy-looking, unopened bottle of malt whisky, opens it and pours himself a hefty measure

There is the sound of the door of Mary's granny-flat opening and shutting from the hall

Mary (*off*) Helen! ... Helen!

John goes into top gear, takes his drink, and zooms off into the kitchen

Mary Ferguson, his mother-in-law, comes into the living-room. She is a widow, in her sixties, a lady who still takes considerable care about a respectable appearance

Helen! ... Helen! (*She looks round the room, registers John's jacket on the chair with surprise, and looks puzzled*) John! (*She glances towards the kitchen, and goes towards it*) John!

John appears in the doorway, still clutching his drink, and looking guilty, a man surrendering

John Hello. I was just getting some ice for my drink.

She looks at his drink, and registers there is no ice in it

About to put it in.

He goes back into the kitchen. There is the sound of the fridge door opening, ice-trays being rattled and the door closing

Mary I thought I heard Helen come in.
John (*off*) No. It was me.

Mary sees spilled papers from the file on the floor. She bends down and starts picking them up

John comes out of the kitchen with his drink, now with ice in it

Don't bother. I'll do that ...

Mary continues to pick them up

(*Irritated*) Please. I'll do it. (*He is forced to pick them up*)

Mary Now she's out all the time Helen should get a cleaning-lady.

John takes all the papers from her, and shoves them all back into their original file

John Did you come in for something?
Mary I've been on my own all day. I thought I heard someone come in-- here.
John (*irritably*) Yes. You did. Me. (*He takes a long swig at his drink, and then looks guilty about his irritability*) Would you like a drink?
Mary Well, as you're having one—just a small one.

He goes over and pours her a very small one

Helen's late again then.
John What else is new? (*He hands her the drink*)
Mary She's working too hard. I heard this programme on the wireless

Act I, Scene 1 3

today—all these working women saying how they worked a seventy-hour week—if you include domestic work. Most men only work a forty-hour week.
John You've been listening to those phone-ins again.
Mary There was this expert—a psychiatrist, who said over half the women in this country were over-tired.
John I wonder how they find the energy to phone in all the time. Anyway most of those phone calls are rigged. They pay a few people to put on different voices.
Mary They don't. There was a woman this morning, just about to have a baby, and she said what with going to work, and going to the clinic, there just wasn't time . . .
John I was just going upstairs to change. Finish your drink. Don't hurry . . .

He makes his escape through the living-room door, taking his jacket with him

Left alone, Mary takes another sip of her drink, and goes over and puts the television on. The sound comes up normally, but Mary's hearing not being all it might be, she turns it up louder. She settles down in front of it, nursing her scotch

The living-room door opens and Helen Bailey comes in. She is an alert, bright-looking woman, a few years younger than her husband. Her trousers and jacket are expensive, and trendily unisex, but not aimed to appear younger than she is. She carries a bulging shoulder-bag

Like John, she also looks as though she has had a hard day. She visibly wilts as the sound of the television, and the sight of her mother ensconced, hits her. Mary doesn't hear her come in

Helen (*shouting*) Hello, Mum. Do you mind? (*She goes over and turns the television off*) What's the matter? Isn't your telly working?
Mary No. It's fine.

She sees Helen is looking at her drink

Oh, John gave me this. I didn't help myself. He went upstairs to change. (*Confidentially*) Not in a very good mood.
Helen He's been having a hard time at work—since the take-over.
Mary I can always tell. He starts criticizing what I listen to on the radio.
Helen Phone-ins.
Mary He'd listen to them too if he was on his own all the time.
Helen No, he'd listen to his old records.

John comes in. He has spruced himself up, and changed his shirt for a more casual one open at the neck

John Hello.
Helen Hello, love. Sorry I'm late. (*She kisses him on the cheek*)
John Good day at the pizza factory?
Helen Chaos. I left Val to cope.

John (*sourly*) About time she did, isn't it?
Helen (*brushing the remark aside*) All our orders were late. The anchovies didn't show up again. They've been on order for two weeks.
Mary I don't like those ones with anchovies.

John goes over to the drinks cabinet to help himself to another drink

John I read somewhere there was a world shortage of anchovies. They've changed their breeding-patterns or something.
Helen Just my luck.
John Do you want one? (*He holds up the fancy scotch bottle*)
Helen Absolutely. (*Noticing the bottle*) Why are we drinking that? It's not Christmas.
John We're out of the cheap stuff. It's been a hard week.
Helen (*concerned*) How was it today?

John glances at Mary. It is not the moment to unburden himself

John Not spectacular. (*He brings the drink over to Helen*)
Mary Nothing spectacular happened here either.
John Were you expecting something to?
Helen (*to Mary*) Didn't you go to the embroidery class?
Mary I told you. It's the holidays still. I don't know why they have such long holidays. It's not as if we're all dropping from exhaustion from doing embroidery every Wednesday afternoon.
Helen I'll put some supper on in a moment.
John Good. I'm starving.
Helen I thought you were having a business lunch with Coleman. Don't say he only bought you sandwiches.
John It was cancelled.
Helen Why?
John (*glancing at Mary*) I'll tell you later.
Mary Oh yes. I remember what I came in to ask you. My oven's still funny. Can't cook anything in it. Can you get someone in to look at it?
Helen I've told you the electrician's coming on Friday.
Mary Ah! (*She stands up*) Well, I'd better be getting along. (*As no invitation to stay is forthcoming, she goes towards the door. She turns back towards John*) By the way, the wallpaper's still coming down in my kitchen.
John I've asked Arthur Hollis to send someone in to redecorate it.
Mary Who?
John Arthur Hollis. You know, Arthur next door.
Mary Ah! I'd better go and put my dinner on. (*Pointedly*) I'm having to fry everything. (*She waits, but no invitation is forthcoming*) It's bad for you — frying. I heard this doctor on the wireless say it was bad for the heart.
John Ah! Well I read they'd decided frying was all right. It's jogging that's bad for you.
Helen Are you doing anything tonight?
Mary No, don't worry. I'm not going jogging. (*A silence, while another invitation doesn't arrive*) I suppose I'll watch television. Not that there's anything worth watching these days.

Act I, Scene 1 5

Mary goes out, leaving the door open. She goes through her own door, on the other side of the hall, banging it behind her

John Did you have to ask her that?
Helen I'm sorry. I'm tired. I wasn't thinking.
John She always says she's doing nothing. The implication is that we sit in here doing something, and she sits on the other side of that wall doing nothing. Guaranteed to create guilt.
Helen You're too sensitive, love. She's my mother, and I can bear it. Would you rather we were driving up North all the time to see she was all right?
John No.
Helen We agreed when she came that we wouldn't let her become dependent.
John When I agreed to a granny-flat, I didn't know she'd be in there like a caged whippet, just waiting for a human sound from in here. A door opening, a cough, a sneeze, and she's in through her door like—an unleashed greyhound.
Helen Make up your mind. Is she a whippet or a greyhound?
John What fascinates me is how she can hear a sneeze through a wall, and half the time she can't hear when she's two inches away from your mouth.
Helen What do you want me to do? Wall her in?
John It's an idea. (*He drains his drink, and suddenly slumps*) Oh God. What a day!
Helen I'll put some supper on. Then we can swop awful days.
John I bet mine was worse than yours. I told you Coleman cancelled the lunch ...

The doorbell rings. They are both startled

Helen Who can that be?
John (*getting up*) Probably Jehovah's Witnesses. Maybe tonight I'll join.

Helen jumps up, a thought striking her with horror

Helen Oh hell. It's Wednesday.
John So?
Helen It's the Hollises. I forgot I asked them round.
John Oh no. Not tonight. I want to talk to you. Let's pretend we're not in.

Helen grabs her bag from the chair

Helen We can't. We cancelled them last time. They'll think we're trying to avoid them.
John You can't avoid Arthur. He lives next door. Sometimes I think he lives on both sides of us.
Helen Hold the fort while I tidy myself up.

There is a double knock on the door

Try and be nice to them.

He gives her a pained smile, and she goes out and rushes upstairs. John goes out to the front door. We hear his voice greeting the Hollises

John (*off*) Hello, Arthur. Hello, Gwen.
Gwen
Arthur } (*off, together*) Hello, John.

Arthur and Gwen Hollis come into the living-room

Arthur is a building-contractor. A burly man in his thirties, with a slight London accent. He wears a check sports-jacket, tan trousers, and an open-necked yellow shirt. Gwen is slightly younger than Arthur. Even though she is only dropping in on the neighbours Gwen has taken some trouble with her hair and make-up, and wears a colourful dress. The effect is of an attractive, but definitely unliberated housewife

John follows them into the room

There is, from the start, a noticeable chill between Arthur and Gwen, as though they have managed to have a row in the short distance between the two front doors

Gwen Not too early, are we?
John No, no. Bang on time.
Arthur Well, it's not far to walk. Managed to persuade Gwen not to take the car.
Gwen Helen is home, isn't she?
John Yes. Just got back.
Gwen I know how busy she's been. I hardly see her anymore.
John Me neither. Rarely see her at breakfast. Never get dinner before nine.
Arthur It's a hard life making money these days.
Gwen Still I envy her. Having her own business, I mean.
Arthur (*pointedly to Gwen*) No point envying people with good ideas, is there? That's what it's all about.
John (*riled*) What about luck?
Arthur Got to be in the right place at the right time.
John What'll you have to drink, Gwen?
Gwen Sherry, please.
John Arthur?
Arthur Scotch, please.

John crosses and pours drinks

John How's the building business going?
Arthur As an engineer you should know. Lousy. Small jobs. Nothing to get your teeth into. *Nouveau* bloody rich putting in extra bathrooms to up their mortgages. If I have to put in another shower-unit or bidet ...
Gwen How's the granny-flat working out, John?
John OK. (*He hands them their drinks*)
Gwen Is she well now?
John Fine, last time I saw her—about three seconds ago.
Gwen We're going to have to do that for my mother soon. Save dragging up to Leicester all the time. It must be so nice for Helen's mum to be able to pop in and out.

Act I, Scene 1   7

John It's got its drawbacks. Cheers.
Arthur
Gwen } (*together*) Cheers.

Helen comes in. She has combed her hair, and freshened up her make-up

Helen Hello. Sorry about that. Had to freshen up.
Gwen (*worried*) You did say Wednesday, didn't you?
Helen Of course. I got home late, that's all.
John Hope you're not starving—like me. Dinner will be delayed, as usual.

Helen flashes him a look, too late

Gwen (*upset*) Oh dear. I've got dinner ready. I thought you'd only asked us for drinks.

There is concealed social embarrassment, for varied reasons, all round

Arthur (*with a smile covering a dig*) Trust Gwen to get arrangements wrong. I reckon we'll probably have Christmas on the wrong day this year.
Helen We did—er—only ask you for drinks. I mean, I—er—haven't put any dinner on yet.
John (*blithely*) Yes, well—ignore me. Never get anything right. (*To Gwen*) We'll celebrate Christmas together—you and me—on the twenty-third. Want a drink, Helen?

She nods

  Drink up. You'd better have another, if it's only drinks. (*He goes to the drinks-cabinet, and pours Helen a scotch*)
Arthur (*to Helen*) How are things with you, Helen? The pizza business booming, eh?
Gwen I think pizza's taken over from Chinese take-away as the national diet.

John brings Helen her drink, and pours more sherry in Gwen's glass

John They keep it a secret that they're very constipating.
Arthur (*to John*) You'll be able to live off her soon. More than I will off Gwen when the old building business packs in.

John takes Arthur's empty glass, and crosses to refill it

Gwen (*combative*) I've told you, I'll go out to work if you get someone to look after the kids, cook and clean ...
Helen (*pacifying, to Arthur*) I didn't start till Tom had left school.
Arthur How is young Tom?

John brings over another scotch to Arthur. He has poured himself another large one too

Helen He's fine. Playing up North at the moment.
Arthur Still in his black leather, is he?
John Oh yes. His Gestapo phase. Except they probably played the guitar better than he does.

Helen That's not fair. He's very good.
John If you don't listen to the sound.
Helen Ignore him. He's just a frustrated jazz-pianist.
Gwen Do you play?
John Only records these days.

There is the sound of Mary's door opening and shutting in the hall

The living-room door opens, and Mary comes in

Mary Sorry. I didn't know you were entertaining.
John We're not. Just a drink.
Mary I want to borrow an onion.
Helen You know Gwen and Arthur—from next door.
Mary Ah, yes. (*Peering at Arthur*) You're going to do my kitchen, aren't you?
Helen (*embarrassed*) Arthur's firm are going to send somebody.
Mary Ah! Well, I hope somebody comes quickly, or it'll all be down. (*To Gwen*) It's very cheap wallpaper, whoever put it up. I'd never put up wallpaper in a kitchen anyway.
Gwen Quite.
Mary When I had my house . . .

Helen gets up quickly

Helen Come and choose an onion.
Mary I think I'll need some margarine too.

She follows Helen into the kitchen

Arthur (*to John*) I'll send someone in next week to do her kitchen.
John (*lowering his voice slightly*) There's one other little thing. Is there someway you could turn a door into a wall?
Arthur Take the door out and brick it up.
John Yes, but you'd have to do it discreetly. It's hers. (*Nodding towards the kitchen*) She's got a door that leads into our hall. If she had to go out through her front door (*his fingers walk*) and come round to ours . . .
Arthur I don't see how I can brick up a door discreetly.
John Well . . . she could have more shelving, or maybe another unit. How about a dishwasher? There'd be space to plumb in a dishwasher. (*Warming to the idea*) Come and have a look.

John and Arthur go out into the granny-flat. Mary comes in from the kitchen, followed by Helen who carries a dish of nuts. Mary carries an onion, some margarine, and a pizza wrapped in cling film

Mary Helen gave me this. Out of her freezer. I don't feel like cooking tonight. Mind you, I don't like to eat these too often, they're very——
Helen Where are John and Arthur?
Gwen They went into the flat.
Mary What did they go in there for?
Gwen (*embarrassed*) John said something about—a dishwasher.

Act I, Scene 1

Mary A dishwasher! I always eat on my own. I have three plates a day to wash. Anyway there's no room for one. (*Firmly*) I don't want a dishwasher.

She goes out and into her flat

Helen John gets some potty ideas. (*Offering nuts*) Have some nuts. I meant to make something to nibble, but I got back late. Work's been chaotic recently.
Gwen It's going well though, isn't it?
Helen All right, but it's still an uphill struggle. I sometimes think I left it too late to go into business.
Gwen Nonsense. I wish I had your energy. I do nothing worthwhile all day, and I'm fagged out by the ten o'clock News. I saw your pizzas in Wilson's the other day.
Helen It's our biggest new retail order.
Gwen I should really find myself something to do. With both kids at school all day now . . .
Helen If you're happy at home why should you?
Gwen Bit like your mum, I suppose. I get lonely.

John and Arthur come back into the living-room

John Got a real flea in our ear, we did.
Helen You weren't trying to have her walled-in, were you?
John No, no. Make a few improvements for her, that's all.
Arthur (*to Helen*) Got a mind of her own, your mum.
Gwen (*to Helen*) She looks really well now. Being here must agree with her.
Helen Yes, but it's been difficult for her readjusting. But then we don't want her to get too dependent on us for company.
John That's why I restrain myself dropping in on her.
Gwen We're going to face that problem with my mum soon. She's been pretty lonely since my dad died.

John seems suddenly hit by the gloom again. He sags in his chair

John Great, isn't it?

They all look at him. He is silent and preoccupied

Helen What?
John What?
Helen What's great?
John I mean us—you spend half your life worrying about your kids—their education, how they're growing up, not doing nasty things after school. Then just when you think you're going to be shot of all that, your dad goes and dies, and you've got your mother to worry about all over again.
Arthur Well, that's life, isn't it?
John (*irritated by Arthur's clichés*) That's right, Arthur. Indubitably.

Arthur gives a quick, angry look at John, knowing he is being sent up. Helen, embarrassed, tries to defuse the situation

Helen Trouble is we're at the sandwich age. I mean kids pressing on one side, old folk on the other. We're like the filling.

This casts gloom on everyone, except Arthur

Arthur I'm not ending up in anyone's sandwich. Cheerful lot, aren't we? Here's what we should do. Knock through between our houses. Put in one dirty great granny-flat. Put our mothers in there together. Then we all piss off and live in Spain.
Gwen You'd be better off knocking through between our lounge and morning-room—like this. (*Gesturing at the room, turning to Helen*) I've always loved this room. I keep telling Arthur we should knock through like this.

Arthur (*wearily*) Yes. She keeps telling me.

Helen We've never really finished it properly. I've always meant to take out that second fireplace. We never seem to have the time to get round to it.

The phone rings. John gets up, and goes to answer it

John (*into the phone*) Hello. . . . (*Wearily*) No, Val, you're not disturbing me. I was in the bath, that's all. . . . No, no. I'll go and see if she's in yet.

Helen is not amused. She gets up and crosses to the phone

(*To Helen*) Guess who?

Helen takes the phone. John crosses back to Arthur and Gwen

Helen (*into the phone*) Hello, Val. . . . No, it's fine. Just got in. . . . Oh, no. Why? . . . (*She listens to a long explanation*)
John (*quietly to Arthur and Gwen*) It's her partner. Whenever Val's left in charge things go wrong. I think she beats the workers.
Helen (*into the phone*) No, no. Just leave it. I'll come in early and do it. . . . It'll be OK. 'Night. (*She puts the phone down*)

John crosses and gets scotch and sherry bottles

(*To Gwen and Arthur*) Sorry about that. Small hiccough at work.

John comes back with the bottles

John Another drink everyone.
Gwen Not for me.
John Just a drop. (*He pours more than a drop*)
Gwen We mustn't stay long. You've got your dinner to think about.
John No thought required there. Fridge stuffed with you-know-what. Fifteen minutes in a hot oven, and, as it says in the ad, prestissimo—the true taste of Italy. (*He pours more scotch into Arthur's glass*)
Arthur What about your constipation, old son?
John They've invented a new variety of pizza. Garnished with anchovy and Senokot, it causes and cures the problem simultaneously.
Helen (*irritated*) John's obsessed with his bowels.

There is another silence, as the marital tension switches between the couples

Gwen (*brightly*) Why don't you come back to us? We've got enough for four. Arthur can eat a little less.
Helen No. Why don't you stay here? If you don't mind eating my pizza.
Arthur Great. (*To Gwen*) We can have your casserole tomorrow.
Gwen Have you got enough for us?
Helen Ask John.
John Yes. Enough for the Italian Army.
Arthur OK. Rather than iron rations at home, we'll eat here. I'll go next door and get some best plonk. Red or white?
Gwen Lash out, Arthur, and bring some of each.
John I've a better idea. Let's go out and have dinner. What about *The San Carlo*? It's near.
Arthur Have you seen their prices recently?
John Don't worry. On my expense-account. It needs bumping up this month.

Helen looks at him suspiciously

Arthur Business must be good. That take-over's been working out for you, has it?

John ignores the question as he crosses to the desk and looks up the number in their phone-book

John Ah. We've got their number. (*He starts to dial*)
Gwen Gosh, I haven't eaten out for ages.
Arthur They probably won't have a table. It's always full, despite their prices.
Gwen How do you know? When did you eat there?
Arthur (*caught out*) Grantley took me there—last month. Very good—but an arm and a leg.
Gwen (*coldly*) Which did you eat?
John (*into the phone*) Hello. Have you got a table for four for this evening? ... (*His hand over the phone, to the others*) They can give us a table if we're there in fifteen minutes.

Helen doesn't look at all keen on the idea, but Gwen is quite excited

Gwen I'd better go and see the kids are all right.
John (*into the phone*) Fine. We'll be there. Bailey's the name. (*He puts the phone down*) All arranged. We'd better move.

Arthur drains his whisky. Gwen abandons her sherry. They stand up and head for the door

Arthur We can go in my car. See you out front.

Arthur and Gwen go

Helen continues looking suspiciously at John

Helen What's got into you?

John holds his glass up to her

John It's good stuff. (*He finishes what is left in his glass*)
Helen Do you know something I don't know?
John (*playing innocent*) What do you mean?
Helen Has Coleman brought in a new building programme?

He comes over and puts his arm round her

John No, but what the hell? We're only young once.
Helen But does it have to be with the Hollises? (*She goes and draws the curtains*)
John Why not? Love thy neighbour—especially if you're not paying for it.
Helen Good idea. I'm starving. It's about time Coleman stood us a treat.

Mary comes through the door. She holds the pizza

Mary I can't have this.
Helen What's wrong with it?
Mary You can't fry pizza, can you?
Helen No. You put it in the oven.
Mary Ah! My oven isn't working. (*Putting them in the wrong*) Remember? I told you.
Helen Oh dear, I forgot. Use our oven.
Mary All right. Then we can all have supper together.
John We're going out to supper.
Helen With the Hollises.
Mary (*disappointed*) Oh!

There is the sound of Arthur's car hooting impatiently outside

John We've got to go.
Helen 'Bye, Mum. Enjoy your supper.

Helen and John go out

Mary stands, looking disconsolately after them. She looks down at the pizza

Mary (*sourly*) And it's got anchovies on it.

Mary goes out into the kitchen

Black-out. Pause, then the Lights come up in the hall

Helen and John come in, back from their dinner out with the Hollises. Helen switches on the main light in the living-room. John follows her in. With more drink aboard, John retains his rather manic good cheer

Helen I'm surprised you and Arthur can still walk.
John I think I'm walking rather well.
Helen Did you have to drink so much?
John No. It just sort of happened.
Helen It happened because you kept ordering more.
John Well—I thought Gwen needed relaxing.
Helen She'd relax if Arthur stopped getting at her all the time.
John Oh, I don't know. I thought she did her bit.
Helen Come on. He asked for it.

Act I, Scene 1 13

John They were both asking—and getting. Maybe that's the basis of their relationship. They probably love each other deeply.
Helen Rubbish. I like Gwen. I feel sorry for her. He's a male chauvinist pig.
John They make the best builders.
Helen And drink the most brandy. Did you have to encourage him?

He goes toward the drinks-cabinet and gets out the scotch bottle

John Want one?
Helen No. And you don't either.
John You're right. (*He puts the bottle down*)
Helen I'll make some coffee. And you should drink some water too.
John No, no. Don't go away. (*He is suddenly serious*)

She looks at him

Helen I'm going away to bed. You too.
John Just a nightcap.
Helen You both had three just-a-nightcaps. I saw the bill. It was bloody outrageous.
John Well, I don't think Our Lord stinted at the Last Supper.
Helen What does that mean?

John looks away from her. He picks up the bottle, and pours himself a drink. Helen watches him suspiciously

John "The time has come, the Walrus said" ... (*He takes a pull at his drink*) I've joined the club.
Helen What club?
John The over three million club. They don't tell you exactly what number you are. (*Pause*) I lost my job.
Helen (*not taking it in*) What?
John Well, I didn't actually lose it—I got fired—sacked—made redundant.
Helen (*aghast*) I don't believe it.

He nods. There is a silence

By Coleman?
John The very same.
Helen But ... oh no. But ... I thought ... you said when they took over he was going to sort things out.
John He did. Very neatly. He stays. I go. That turned out to be one of the conditions of the take-over. They get a skeleton company. I'm the discarded flesh. Mind you, Coleman put it more delicately than that. I think he said something about slimming-down, paying one's way, having to earn one's keep. Made it sound quite patriotic. I think they send out a standard speech from the PM's office, and Coleman memorized it. (*He goes and slumps on a chair, puts his drink down*)

Helen is still standing, stunned

Helen (*angrily*) The two-faced ... (*She controls herself, comes over and puts her arms round him*) Oh God, I'm sorry. I'm sorry. When did you find out?

John He told me instead of taking me to lunch.

Helen Why didn't you tell me before?

John Wasn't a chance, was there? Not the sort of news you want an audience for. I was waiting for the right moment.

Helen (*shutting her eyes*) That's terrible, love. You built that place up. How could he?

John (*ignoring the question*) I rehearsed what I'd say on the way home. Not easy to tell your wife you've lost your job. At one point I even thought of not telling you at all. Some people don't, you know. Kiss their wives goodbye in the morning then go and sit in the park. Come back at six-thirty. Kiss wifey again. (*Doing wifey voice*) "Good day at the office, dear?" (*Hubby's voice*) "Not bad, not bad. Nothing spectacular."

Helen (*very upset*) Stop it, love. (*She is near tears, picks up his glass of scotch, and takes a quick gulp*) I still can't believe that swine didn't give you any indication he was going to get rid of you.

John Well, he didn't. He's a businessman, sent in to cut costs. There wasn't enough work to go round. So that's it. This morning an engineering consultant, this evening a ... (*He takes the glass from her, and takes a swig himself*) Maybe I'll be on the nine o'clock news tomorrow. One of those flashing blobs on the map—twelve hundred jobs gone in Gateshead, seven hundred in Skegness, one in Moorgate.

Helen I still can't believe ... (*A shock thought hits her. She pulls away from him*) Good God, you mean you've just spent a hundred and eight pounds of your own money taking the Hollises to dinner?

John takes her hand appeasingly

John No. It's Wednesday. I'm still with the company till Friday. It was Coleman's last supper. I wish Arthur had drunk the whole bottle of brandy.

Helen looks relieved, and manages a pained, but affectionate smile. She sits down, and stares miserably into space

Don't worry. I'll find something else. Meanwhile thank God for the pizza business. I'll never say they're constipating again.

Helen (*drily*) Thanks.

John I'll sing their laxative qualities from the hilltops.

Helen Maybe we ought to go to bed first. Come on.

She takes his hand, and he gets up

We'll talk in the morning. Oh damn, I've got to go in early.

John By the way, I don't think I'll tell your mother for a bit.

Helen Why not?

John She'd probably phone up one of those programmes. Start going on about the unemployment and her poor son-in-law. I'll just tell her I'm changing jobs.

Helen Sometimes you act as though she's your mother, not mine. Why do you always have to have her approval?

John Maybe it's because she's the only mother I've got.

Helen Come on. I'm whacked. You must be too.

She starts to go with him to the door. He breaks away from her

John I'll be up in a sec.
Helen You're not going to drink any more?
John No. I'll just dab it on the wounds.

Helen takes her bag and goes out

John picks up his drink and takes a thoughtful sip. He goes to the desk, and takes his executive diary out of his briefcase. He looks up a phone number, and then dials it, as he did at the beginning of the scene

(*Into the phone*) Oh good, it's you. . . . (*Friendly and charming*) It's John Bailey. Sorry if I'm disturbing you. . . . No, no, there's nothing you can do for me, Mr Coleman. It's just something I forgot to mention before I left the office today. Been on my mind ever since. You're a total shit. Goodnight. (*He puts the phone down, a contented smile on his face*)

Black-out

SCENE 2

The same. Some weeks later. Morning

The living-room is slightly more messy than when we last saw it. Newspapers and journals are spread out on the sofa. On the desk is a large map of Greater London pasted to a board with small red and blue squares stuck on it, as well as some complex looking charts and graphs showing job availabilities and applications

When the Lights come up John is entering various facts and figures on to one of the charts. He is dressed for a job-interview in his snappiest-looking suit, and a much brighter shirt and tie. The Oscar Peterson recording of "On A Clear Day" is playing on the hi-fi. It will become apparent that John only listens to Fifties and Sixties jazz, mainly in piano and small group arrangements. He crosses to the sofa, and looks up a job ad in the Civil Engineer. *He brings it back to the desk, and enters up the salary details, address etc., on one of his very scientific-looking charts. The doorbell rings*

John turns off the hi-fi, and goes out to answer the front door. He comes back into the room with Gwen. She wears jeans and a shirt, and carries a small shopping-bag

Gwen I got what you wanted.
John You're an angel. I just couldn't leave the phone this morning.
Gwen Did it ring?
John Yes.
Gwen The call you wanted?
John No.
Gwen (*getting items out of the shopping-bag*) Butter, eggs, washing-powder.

John Thanks a million. It's hell trying to get a job, run a home, find the right washing-powder.

Gwen takes the three items out to the kitchen

John finishes off an entry on his chart

Gwen comes out of the kitchen, and takes in his appearance

Gwen You look very smart this morning.
John The younger image.
Gwen What time's the interview?
John Two-thirty.
Gwen Which one's this?
John Civil Engineering consultants in Victoria. Second time round. I was short-listed.
Gwen I'll keep my fingers crossed.
John Main competition I reckon comes from an Australian rugby type. Thrustful, dynamic. Six foot five. Enormous hands. No dress sense and shifty eyes. I'm going to play it my way—sincere, medium height, eye-to-eye contact.
Gwen He doesn't stand a chance.
John He's thirty-five.

She looks at the map, mass of charts and papers

Gwen What's all this?
John It's a full-time job getting a job. It's amazing what you discover when you get organized. For instance ... (*he points to coloured red spots on the map*) ... in the Greater London area there are currently three civil engineering jobs worth having.
Gwen Only three?
John That's at my salary and seniority level. If I come down four thousand pounds a year and take luncheon vouchers, I can push the number up to twelve. (*He points to blue blobs on the map*)
Gwen How many have you applied for?

He shows her a complex chart of names and coloured lines

John Eight. Directly for three. Five through the executive agency. So far three total turn-downs, two on grounds of over-qualification. In three I'm through to the quarter finals, and in two through to the semi-finals.
Gwen I think you'll make it to Wembley.
John There's my age.
Gwen It's a nice age.
John On the employment market it's over the hill. I've met some others like me on the job-circuit, flogging themselves round the track, a bit old for sprinting. Used to be in nice, secure jobs. Thought they could let up a bit, put their feet up, with a nice pension at the end. Instead we're out on the street, shoving our c.v.s under everyone's door. I suppose some of us may never work again.
Gwen Oh, come on. You'll be all right. I've read engineers are in demand.

John Depends what sort. If I was electronic or mechanical, no problem. But who wants a civil engineer?

Gwen What about all those things you do? You build roads, bridges ...

John Schools, hospitals. There isn't the money for luxuries like that any more. These days it's micro-chip or nothing.

Gwen I wouldn't know a micro-chip if I fell over one.

John But that's what it's all about. Everything can leak, rot, or fall down. The potholes will take over, but as long as we've got computer-games ... (*He does an impersonation of a moron playing a computer game*)

Mary comes into the room and registers Gwen with surprise

Mary Oh, hello. I thought I heard Helen come back.

John She isn't normally back at lunchtime.

Mary Well, I never know who's going to be in these days. Did you get my eggs?

Gwen I got them.

Mary That's very kind of you.

Gwen I'll fetch them.

Gwen goes out into the kitchen

Mary (*to John*) When's your new job start?
John Soon.

Gwen comes out of the kitchen with half a dozen eggs

Mary (*to John*) I've got the electricity man coming this afternoon. Will you be here?

John No.

Mary My bill for the last quarter was a hundred and fourteen pounds. There's something wrong with my meter, but they'll never admit it. If you were there he might explain.

John I've got a meeting.

Mary With your new job?

John (*embarrassed in front of Gwen*) Yes.

Gwen (*to Mary*) Perhaps I can help. Why don't you call me when he arrives?

Mary They never come when they say they're coming. They wait till you're out, and then creep up and shove a note through your door to say they've been. I was listening to a programme yesterday. A man phoned in about gas and electricity charges ...

The phone rings

John He phones everybody. (*He answers the phone*)

Gwen hands Mary her eggs

(*Into the phone*) Oh, hello, Mr Goodison. ... No, I'm going to Dawson, McVeagh at two-thirty. Second ... er ... meeting ...

Mary (*to Gwen*) I do wish he'd start his new job soon. It isn't good for a man to be around the house all day ... and with Helen out all the time ...

Gwen nods

John (*covering the mouthpiece and hissing at them*) Sssh! (*Into the phone*) Fine. I could make tomorrow at eleven. . . . They know I'm not interested in going to Kuwait, don't they? . . . As long as they accept that, I suppose it's worth a try. Right. Many thanks. (*He puts the phone down*)

Mary This new job isn't sending you to Kuwait, is it?

John No, Mary. I said they'd have *to wait*—till my new office is ready.

Mary Ah! (*To Gwen*) Thanks for these. I just fancied an egg for lunch, and I thought John was going out shopping. Not that eggs taste like eggs any more. All from those terrible battery chickens.

Gwen These are free-range—from the butcher.

Mary Well, I suppose at least that means they allow the chickens to walk about. You have to pay extra for that, don't you?

John (*exasperated*) The eggs are on me. Enjoy your lunch.

Mary (*to Gwen*) Goodbye then.

Mary goes out, clutching her free-range eggs

John We should have walled her in when we could afford it.

Gwen You haven't told her yet—about the job?

John I'm not bloody going to either. Can you imagine how she'd cluck around me?

Gwen Free-ranging. Well, I'd better get back to the chores. What are you doing about lunch? Oh dear, I suppose all mothers sound the same.

John It's OK. I've washed behind my ears, and got my c.v. ready.

Gwen C.v.?

John picks up a sheaf of his c.v.s from the desk

John Curriculum vitae. An exercise in depressing yourself. My whole life reduced to one-page, double spacing. And very boring it sounds too.

Gwen Mine wouldn't even make a page.

John You have to exaggerate a bit. Everybody does. All those things nobody can really check. (*Pointing at part of his c.v.*) I spent three weeks on a course in Germany once. I said it was six months. Makes me sound more cosmopolitan. Into Europe and all that. (*He looks at his watch*) I'd better get moving or I'll be late.

Gwen You'd better have some lunch if you want to beat that Australian giant.

John Never eat before an interview. Hunger gives one an edge.

Gwen Good luck then.

John Thanks.

Gwen picks up her shopping-bag, and goes out

John collects up some papers and c.v.s and puts them in his briefcase. He crosses to the wall-mirror, adjusts his tie, and pats down his hair. He straightens himself up, shoulders back, chin out, and gives himself a direct, sincere look in the mirror. He modifies it slightly so it is less aggressively sincere. As an afterthought, he cups his hands over his mouth, breathes out, and checks his breath is fresh. He seems satisfied

Act I, Scene 2								19

He turns, picks up his briefcase turns to go, and stops at the drinks-cabinet. He firmly touches the wood of the cabinet twice, and goes out

Black-out. Joe Pass recording of "Nice Work If You Can Get It" plays

Scene 3

The same. Some days later. Morning

When the Lights come up Helen, dressed for work, comes out of Mary's flat, carrying some dirty towels

Helen It's all right. I'll put these in my washing machine. (*She dumps the towels on the sofa, and crosses back to the table and sits to finish off some sums on her pocket calculator. She cannot use the desk as it is cluttered with John's stuff*)

The phone rings. She gets up to answer it

John comes in through the living-room door like greased lightning, and beats her to the phone. He wears a tracksuit, and looks anxious and dishevelled

John (*into the phone*) Hello.... (*His voice drops*) Oh, Val.... Yes. She's here. I'll get her. (*He puts the phone down*) Your partner again.
Helen Can't you at least be civil to her?
John No. Not this morning. It's hard at the best of times.

Helen takes a blue folder from the table over to the desk and picks up the phone

John goes out

Helen (*into the phone*) Hello.... They've finally arrived. Thank God. Only a month late.... I suppose there's no reason why Japanese anchovies shouldn't be as good as Portuguese ones.... In what way different?... I don't know what a live anchovy looks like....

From the front of the house John can be heard shouting at someone

John (*off*) Whichever it is, it gets later every day.
Helen Yes, I've just done the figures. I make it seventeen thousand, five hundred less the loan interest.... Not bad, is it? I'll take them into Dubois on my way in. Should be with you by around twelve. See you then. (*She puts the phone down, and crosses back to the table, leaving her blue folder on the desk*)

John comes in through the living-room door, holding the morning's thin suppply of mail

Who were you shouting at then?
John The postman. He's never here before ten.
Helen Why don't you complain to the Post Office? (*Looking anxious, she starts packing her papers into her shoulder bag*)

John What about? He's a clever bugger our postman. Said it wasn't the first delivery that was late, it was the second delivery that was early. (*He puts the letters down on the desk as though he doesn't want to know about them. He flourishes a postcard at her*) Card from Tom.
Helen Where from?
John (*looking*) Huddersfield. The Civic Centre in sunshine. (*Scanning the card*) He wowed them there last Saturday.
Helen When's he ever going to play south of Leeds?
John They're probably more musically tolerant up there.

Helen gestures at the rest of the mail

Helen (*pointedly*) What else?

John grimaces

Dawson, McVeagh?

He nods

Aren't you going to open it?
John I think I need a drink first.
Helen Take a deep breath. Be better for you.

John takes a letter from the pile watched apprehensively by Helen. He slits the envelope open, gets the letter out and reads it. His shoulders sag

No?
John (*reading*) "The directors of Dawson, McVeagh thank me for my trouble, and hope I will reclaim any expenses involved in coming to the interviews."
Helen (*upset*) That's rotten. I'm sorry.
John (*angrily crumbling letter*) It means they gave it to that giant git from Down Under.
Helen The one with bad breath?
John No. He was Scots. This sod had shifty eyes, and frightening great hands. Maybe they're trying to save on equipment. Use him instead of a crane.
Helen What does that leave?
John Cunningham's. The rest's rubbish. (*Pause*) Great for the confidence, isn't it?
Helen Maybe the salary-level was the problem.

He grunts

When will you hear from Cunningham's?
John Goodison at the Agency should phone about that this morning, if bloody Val doesn't keep tying up the line. She can't decide what tights to put on without calling you.
Helen She called to say the anchovies had finally arrived.
John (*sourly*) Terrific!
Helen I knew you'd be pleased. They're important to us. Don't knock them.
John Would I knock a poor little anchovy! (*Singing*) "Fish got to swim, birds got to fly" ... (*Speaking*) Just don't bring any home. I loathe the little brown buggers.

Helen Bad news makes you manic.

John It's not all bad news. (*He takes another letter in an official brown envelope and slits it open*) The Department of Employment to the rescue. Welcome to the club. My first dole cheque. (*He takes out the cheque and looks at it*)

Helen How much?

John Twenty-eight pounds and forty-five p. per week.

Helen Is that all?

John I'm not allowed supplementary benefit because you're earning. And this will be taxed.

Helen But surely not much?

John They'll find a way. I have to declare it jointly with your income. I've thrown myself on the compassion of the State, and they've kicked me in the balls. They've buggered up the economy, *I* pay for it. Ah well, pay this into our dwindling account.

Helen I'm not going to the bank. Can't you?

John No. I can't face the cashiers. Especially our Miss Phipps. Can't you imagine her sorrowing look when she sees where the cheque comes from?

Helen All right. (*She takes the cheque*) Be a love and dump those in the washing-machine. I'll do it all tonight. I shouldn't be back late. Did you ask Pullen's to deliver?

John No, I'll go and collect it all—when I'm jogging. It can be my handicap, running home with a chicken and three pounds of minced beef.

Helen picks up her shoulder bag, and looks at him, concerned

Helen What are you doing today?

John Don't worry about me.

Helen You're not going to hang around all day just waiting for a phone-call?

John No.

Helen You always said if you ever had time you'd do a few things around the house.

John I'm not hauling out that fireplace, if that's what you mean.

Helen Start small, love—the wallpaper in my mother's kitchen.

John (*irritated*) You're starting to sound like an occupational therapist.

Helen I'm sorry, but ... Look, I know this is all horrible for you, but it's no good just hanging around. Go into town, have lunch with somebody.

John I'll be all right. I've got my eight gramophone records. Have a good day.

Helen goes out. There is the sound of the front door opening and shutting

John stands still, looking after her. He looks disconsolately round the room. It is the moment, shared by all housewives, when the breadwinner has left for work and his, or her, partner wonders how to get through the rest of the day. He goes over to the hi-fi and selects a tape, puts it in and presses the play-button. It is Errol Garner playing "Dreamy"

He crosses towards the kitchen. En route, he picks up the dirty towels from the sofa and takes them out into the kitchen. John returns to the living-room carrying a carpet-sweeper and a duster

He puts them down and looks at his watch. He glances at the phone, and then decides against making a call. He uses the carpet-sweeper on the carpet. As he sweeps over beside the phone he can no longer resist the temptation. He grabs the phone and dials a number, sitting down

    (*Into the phone*) Hello. Mr Goodison, please. ... John Bailey. ... (*He realizes he won't be able to hear over the hi-fi. He puts the phone down, races over and turns the volume down slightly. He goes back to the phone*) Hello ... (*There is no-one there yet*) ... Oh, hello, Mr Goodison. I thought I ought to tell you I've heard from Dawson, McVeagh. I'm afraid it's a "no" ... I was just wondering if you'd heard from Cunningham's yet. ... (*Expectantly*) Ah! ... (*His face falls*) But I told them I was prepared to ... Yes. All right. ... (*Forcing himself*) Has anything else come up? ... Well, I'm still at the same number — for the time being.

He puts the phone down. For a moment he looks desperate as he listens to the music in the background, close to tears. He lets his fingers play an imaginary piano on the table. He gets a grip on himself, picks up the duster, and stands up. The doorbell rings

    He shoves the duster in his pocket and goes out to the front door

    (*Off*) Hello.
Gwen (*off*) Are you busy?
John (*off*) No. Come in.

Gwen comes into the living-room, John follows her in

Gwen wears trousers and a shirt, and carries a large shopping-basket. She registers that John is upset. Her attitude is casual and cheerful, very much one housewife calling on another for elevenses. She looks at the carpet-sweeper and the duster sticking out of his tracksuit pocket

Gwen You're running late this morning. I've done all my chores.
John Distractions.
Gwen (*nodding*) Mary?
John No, not today. It's Wednesday. She has her embroidery class in the afternoon, so she spends the morning unpicking the mess she made of it last week.
Gwen Poor dear. My mother's started going to bridge-classes. She's hopeless at cards. Still I suppose you've got to do something when you've got the whole day on your hands.
John Quite.

Gwen realizing her gaffe, is embarrassed, but flounders further

Gwen I mean — it's not funny growing old.
John I know. What do you want me to do then — bridge or embroidery?
Gwen We are in high spirits this morning, aren't we? (*She looks at him, concerned, but he isn't forthcoming*) I'm just going shopping. Do you or Mary need anything? Seems daft for us all to make separate trips.
John Thanks, but I need the air. I'll get everything when I go jogging.

Act I, Scene 3 23

Gwen I should jog.
John Have a coffee instead.
Gwen OK. I'll make it. (*Gesturing at the carpet-sweeper*) You finish. (*She puts the shopping-basket down by the sofa*)
John No. I don't like anyone else in my kitchen. Put your feet up. The kettle's just been on.

He goes out into the kitchen

Gwen uses the carpet-sweeper on the floor, and then goes to the kitchen door

Gwen I really should jog with you. Or rather behind you. I could never keep up. Have you ever tried yoga?
John (*off*) No.
Gwen It's very good for you. Relaxing. I go to a class at the Institute. Friday afternoons. You ought to come.

John comes out with two mugs of coffee

John I don't have the leotards.
Gwen A tracksuit would do fine.
John I'd rather go to embroidery with my mother-in-law. (*He hands her a mug*)
Gwen Did you sugar it?
John Yes. One lump, one sweetener.

Gwen crosses to the sofa, sits down, and drinks some coffee

Gwen Do you need fruit and veg. today?
John Yes.
Gwen You ought to try the Greek place on the Parade. It's half the price of Wilson's.
John I'll try them.
Gwen They've got good eggs too. (*She sips her coffee*) It's funny.
John It's instant.
Gwen Not the coffee. Dropping in like this—for elevenses. I used to do it with Helen before she started working. You'd just moved in. It was your Tom's last year at school.

John grunts, saddened by the whole thought

Heard about those jobs yet?
John Which ones?
Gwen The two semi-finals.
John I didn't make it to Wembley.
Gwen Oh dear, I'm sorry.
John Not your fault. It was the cretins who interviewed me. I don't think they were used to talking to people born before nineteen fifty.
Gwen Come on. That's only two down. You're up for others, aren't you?
John Not at my kind of salary.
Gwen But you'd accept less, wouldn't you, if it was a good opportunity?

John At one interview last week I offered to forego the pension, do without a desk, make the tea.

Gwen Have you ever thought of going in with Helen?

John I knew someone would ask that sooner or later.

Gwen Well?

John You haven't met her partner Val. A ... dragon.

Gwen Helen must get on with her.

John She does. Val only hates men.

Gwen (*shocked*) Oh!

John Of course, Helen says it's only since her husband walked out one night with all the furniture.

Gwen And now she hates *all* men?

John Give or take an armchair or two, yes.

Gwen Cheer up. Something good will turn up soon. It's not like you're never going to get another job, is it? I mean the recession will lift. It will, won't it?

John You're a real Job's comforter, you are.

Gwen I am? (*Pause*) I've never known what that is.

John Someone who doesn't offer much comfort.

Gwen Well, be careful. At least I know what happened to Job in the end.

John What did happen to him?

Gwen He was swallowed by a whale.

John That was Jonah.

Gwen Oh yes, that's right. What happened to Job?

John I don't know. I must look it up. These days it would be worth knowing. (*He sits on the sofa*)

They drink their coffee

Gwen You and Helen are managing, aren't you? Financially, I mean.

John They won't be making a TV documentary about us, scavenging in dustbins, if that's what you mean.

Gwen You got a — a golden handshake, didn't you? Tide you over?

John Not exactly golden. Chrome. Tarnished chrome.

Gwen But you get the dole too, don't you?

John Oh yes. An absolute fortune. I reckon I'm contributing about twenty quid a week to running the place. For the rest I'm pimping off Helen.

Gwen I'm sure she doesn't mind. Not for a while.

John I'm living off the true taste of Italy.

Gwen Without that you'd really be in trouble.

John Maybe that's what makes it worse. Robs the situation of its tragic dimension. Nothing very tragic about a self-pitying pimp is there?

She reaches out and puts a reassuring hand on his arm

Gwen Don't get sour. Not about Helen. You must admit the pizzas were a good idea.

John She gets lots of good ideas. I don't. As an engineer you get used to solving other people's problems, not your own.

Gwen I think you're jealous.
John Probably.
Gwen Well I think it's terrific—what she's done.
John No, you don't.

She takes her hand away

Gwen Of course I do.
John Rubbish. You hate her for it.
Gwen (*nervously*) No, I don't.
John Yes, you do. Everyone going on about how marvellous Helen is. How successful she's been.
Gwen Well, it's true, isn't it?
John I bet Arthur never stops reminding you about it. Why don't you have a good idea? Why don't you go out and make twenty thousand a year?
Gwen (*reluctant, struggling*) Yes. Well, women like Helen do make women like me feel a bit inadequate. Arthur thinks she's marvellous, of course.
John I know. I've heard him.
Gwen I suppose he thinks if I did that he could loll around all day doing nothing.
John Like me.
Gwen No, I didn't mean that. I mean, you know, at least you liked your work, didn't you?
John Most of the time.
Gwen Arthur doesn't like his any more. He hates it. (*Finishes her coffee*) He despises the people he works for. You've heard him going on about the *nouveau riche*, and immigrants, and how no-one pays their bills on time. He's really changed recently. He comes home in a filthy mood, and takes it out on me. (*She sniffs unhappily*) He takes what I do for granted—the kids, cooking, cleaning, shopping. All he wants is for me to look sexy at supper-time.

She has started to cry. He moves over and puts a hand on her arm

John At least Helen doesn't care what I look like at supper-time.

She looks for her handkerchief to wipe her eyes. She can't find one. John reaches for his, and produces the duster

Gwen It's OK. (*Wiping her eyes with the back of her hand*) Nowadays he seems to enjoy making me feel inadequate. He'd like me to have invented frozen peas or something.
John Helen's made it hard for both of us. The first year her company made a profit was the first year mine made a loss.
Gwen (*still in her own miseries*) I think Arthur would respect me more if I was an office-temp instead of a housewife.

He puts a comforting arm round her

John He'd miss his supper though.

She rests her head on his shoulder

Gwen God, I've come to hate cooking.
John I'm not enjoying it much either.
Gwen Half the time he doesn't notice what I've cooked.
John Helen says I over-cook everything.
Gwen And I never get a thank-you.
John I don't over-cook everything. She's always late.
Gwen Arthur too.

They are a hair's breadth away from a passionate kiss but John pulls away

John Shall we go shopping?
Gwen (*vehemently*) Oh God, I hate shopping. I hate shopping. (*She turns away from him, thumping the cushion with her fist in anger*) I hate it. Hate it. Hate it.
John Me too.

She turns and buries her head on his shoulder

Gwen Oh God!
John What?
Gwen Instead of shopping, couldn't we go upstairs?

John looks stunned. He gets up, moves away from her, his back to the audience. After a beat, Gwen gets up

Gwen (*miserably*) Oh God, I'm sorry. I'm sorry. That was dreadful. Look, forget I ...

She goes towards the door. John's hand is held out to her. She takes it and they go out and upstairs

After several beats, the Lights change slightly. There is the sound of the front door opening and shutting

Helen comes in. She is dressed as she was when she left earlier, and carries her sling shoulder bag

She looks round for signs of John, then crosses to the desk and picks up the blue file she has forgotten. As Helen is putting the file in her bag she spots the two mugs on the coffee-table. She puts the bag down, and goes over to the coffee-table. She picks up Gwen's mug, noticing the lipstick. Then she spots the shopping-basket by the sofa. Helen frowns, puts the mug down, and crosses to the basket. She bends down and pulls a purse out of the basket. She opens it, glances inside, and establishes that it belongs to Gwen. For a brief instant, she looks shocked and angry. She puts the purse back in the basket. She goes quickly toward the door, as though she is about to go up to the bedroom. She goes out into the hall, glances towards the stairs, and then changes her mind. She comes back into the room and pauses, at a loss for a moment

Mary's door opens in the hall. Mary comes through, and into the living-room

Mary Hello. I thought I heard you come in. Shouldn't you be at work?

Helen tries to look and talk calmly. At the same time, she tries to keep her own and Mary's voice down, not to disturb the couple upstairs

Helen (*in a lowered voice*) I came back because I forgot something.
Mary What?
Helen I forgot something.
Mary Why are you whispering?
Helen (*edgy, in a louder voice*) I'm not. It's your hearing. I've told you to get it checked.
Mary There's nothing wrong with it. I can hear perfectly well when people speak distinctly.
Helen I am speaking distinctly.
Mary Yes. You are now.

It is all too much for Helen, who is losing her cool. She picks up her shoulder bag

Helen I'm going to be late for an appointment.
Mary Is John in?
Helen I don't know.
Mary Where is he?
Helen (*sharply*) I don't know. I don't ask him what he's doing every day.

Mary is clearly upset by Helen's tone to her

Mary Well, I only asked.
Helen I'm late. I'll see you this evening. (*She goes impatiently to the door*)
Mary (*on her dignity*) I mightn't be in this evening.
Helen Oh? Where are you going?
Mary (*haughtily*) If you don't ask John, there's no need to ask me.

Helen goes out into the hall and shuts the front door very quietly behind her. Mary, clearly upset by Helen's behaviour, shakes her head, and goes slowly out of the living-room, into the hall, and back into her flat

Fade to Black-out

Scene 4

The same. A few days later. Early evening

When the Lights come up Helen is opening a fresh bottle of whisky by the drinks-cabinet. She is dressed for a formal night out, in a rather severe but chic black and white outfit. The myopic might mistake her for a female maître d'hôtel. She pours herself a drink

Mary comes out of the kitchen, carrying a bottle of milk

Mary I meant to ask the milkman to leave me more this morning. You've still got a pint left. (*She looks uncertainly at Helen's get-up*) That's ... unusual. Is it new?
Helen No. I bought it last year. Wore it on New Year's Eve, remember?
Mary Dear, I forgot the milkman this morning. I don't remember last year. Where are you going?
Helen The Catering Association Dinner.
Mary Ah! (*Pause*) Why are you going there?
Helen I'm in the pizza-business, remember? That's catering.
Mary Oh, yes. How nice! (*Pause*) You're taking John, aren't you?
Helen If he can get himself ready in time. We're being picked up.
Mary You ought to take him out more. He seems very depressed. He has got this new job, hasn't he?

Helen nods

He says his new office isn't ready for him yet.
Helen (*going along with it*) It'll be ready soon.
Mary It's not good for him just to potter round the house. (*Pause*) I caught him reading the Bible the other day.
Helen The Bible?
Mary I've never seen him reading the Bible before, have you?
Helen No.
Mary He said he was reading the Book of Job.
Helen He probably said job—a book about jobs.
Mary I'm not that deaf. He said Job. (*She shakes her head*) He ought to go out more. (*She turns to go*)

John comes in. He is wearing a dinner-jacket and trousers, and a dress-shirt with the collar open. He looks weary and dejected, every inch a man who doesn't want to go out in a dinner-jacket

(*To John*) I needed some more milk.
John But I got you more this morning. You put it in your fridge.
Mary (*admiring him*) That's better than that old tracksuit. You look nice. (*Pause*) Aren't you going to wear a tie?
John I can't find it.
Helen It's with your other ties.
John It's not. I've looked. (*He notices the new bottle of scotch*) Where did that come from?
Helen I just bought it.
John On office-expenses, I hope. (*He goes and helps himself to a glass like a man who has been missing his whisky*)
Mary (*to John*) You were reading the Book of Job, weren't you? The other day?
John Yes. Cheers. (*He drinks*)
Mary (*to Helen*) There! (*To John*) Helen wouldn't believe me.
Helen To cheer yourself up, no doubt.
John No. Actually it was something Gwen said.
Helen I didn't know she was a biblical scholar.

John She was round here for coffee the other day. It's an amazing story—Job, I mean.
Helen Good. Now find your tie, or we'll be late.
Mary God punished him with boils. I remember that. (*To John*) Why did he?
John Totally arbitrary. Satan made this bet with God. Said to God I bet you that if old Job had really rotten luck he'd turn against you.
Mary And then he gave Job boils?
John No. That was just the final little touch. First he lost five hundred oxen and five hundred asses.

John launches into the story as if to stall going out. Helen, seeing the performance for what it is, reacts in an irritated and impatient manner. Only Mary listens with interest

Then a fire came and consumed all his sheep and servants. The Chaldeans, or some such, then came and took all his camels. (*To Helen*) Do you think it's all a parable for the recession? (*He tops up his drink*)
Helen Yes. I'm sure it is. Now could you finish getting dressed? We're going to be late.
John (*ignoring her; to Mary*) He had seven sons and three daughters. They were all having dinner and a wind came, and blew the house in on them. All killed—phut! (*He drinks*)
Mary And *then* he got boils?
John (*nodding*) Smote with sore boils—all over.
Mary And then his friends came. (*Brightly*) Job's comforters. (*She looks at them, delighted to show off her knowledge*) I remember that from Sunday School.
John And they had wonderful names. Eliphaz the ... something or other.
Mary Oh, I don't remember those.
John They had terrific names. (*Seized with his new biblical fervour, he rushes over to the bookshelf, and gets the Bible down. He has left the marker in, and quickly turns to the page*)

Helen is trying hard, in front of her mother, to suppress her irritation at John's time-wasting tactics

Helen It doesn't matter about their names now.
John Here they are. (*Reading from the Bible*) "Eliphaz the Temanite, and Bildad the Shuhite, and Zophar the Naamathite. They came from afar to comfort him, and when they saw him ... (*reading with feeling*) ... they wept, and they rent every one his mantle, and threw dust upon their heads towards heaven."

He throws imaginary dust in the air. Helen turns away angrily. John directs the last bit towards Mary

"So they sat down with him upon the ground seven days and seven nights, and none spoke a word unto him; for they saw that his grief was very great."

John shuts the book. Mary looks disconcerted by him, and thinks hard for something to say

Mary Well friends wouldn't do that for you these days.
Helen All right, now we know why you've turned against God, will you go and find your bow-tie.

Clutching the Bible, John turns his new-found fervour on them again

John That's just the point. Job never turned against God. That's how Satan lost his bet. What Job is really saying to God is "Why me?". And God is saying to Job "Why not you?". There you have the story of all human tragedy.

Mary stares at him as though he is a little touched. Helen isn't impressed by his over-acting

Helen Would you rather stay in tonight and read the Bible?
John I've told you. I can't find my tie. It's vanished.
Helen How could it vanish?
John Maybe Tom took it.
Helen Why would he take it?
John How should I know? Maybe to play a gig or something.
Helen They don't wear bow-ties with black leather. (*Sniffing*) What's that smell? (*To Mary*) Can't you smell it?
John (*sniffing*) It's something burning in the kitchen. (*He gestures at the kitchen*)
Mary (*alarmed*) Oh dear, it's my supper.

Mary rushes out into the hall and through her door. Helen puts her glass down and rushes out after her

John remains, unperturbed. He has finished his drink. He picks up Helen's half-finished one, and puts his empty glass down in its place. He goes over to the hi-fi and selects a record. He puts on Art Tatum playing "Somebody Loves Me", and starts playing the desk

Helen comes back into the living-room with a burned-out saucepan

Helen We could have all gone up in smoke. Oh God, you're not going to sit there drinking and playing music. (*She turns the hi-fi off*)
John (*shrugging, fatalistic*) Can't come to the Caterers' Ball. Haven't got a tie. Too late to buy one anywhere.
Helen It'll be in one of your drawers. You never look properly.
John I haven't worn this monkey-suit for a year. The tie's gone and the socks. (*He raises his trousers to show he is wearing red socks*)
Helen I'll look.

She shoves the burned-out saucepan at him. He takes it, and she goes towards the door

John Fine, but you won't find it.

She turns back, just about holding her temper

Act I, Scene 4

Helen It doesn't seem to matter to you that this dinner is important to me professionally...
John That's irrelevant. I haven't got a tie. Do you want me to come in an open-necked shirt, and look like I run a fish-and-chippo?
Helen I'll paint one on your shirt if we have to. (*Appeasingly*) Look, love, I know what's bothering you. You might sit next to someone who'll ask you what you do. That's it, isn't it?
John The thought occurs.
Helen You're a civil engineer. That's what you are, isn't it? They're not going to know you've lost your job.
John Why don't I go the whole hog—tell them I run Trust House Forte?
Helen Because *he's* going to be there. I'm going to find your tie.

Helen goes out. He takes the burned-out saucepan into the kitchen

After a pause, the front door is heard opening and closing and Tom comes in through the living-room door. He carries an electric guitar-case, and a duffel-bag. He is late teenage, and not at all what previous descriptions have led one to imagine. Instead of black leather, he now wears clean, faded pink jeans, his white top, open at the neck, is closer to a blouse than a shirt. He wears a chunky silver chain, and one ear-ring. His hair looks as if it is in the process of growing-out from being shaved, and is peroxide blond. When he speaks his accent is nothing like his parents'. It is a synthesized mixture, part cultured, part South London. As is common to his musical generation, Tom's identity hasn't quite come together yet

John comes out of the kitchen. He shows double surprise—the sudden appearance of Tom, and Tom's appearance

Tom Hi, Dad.
John Tom? (*He bites back any comment about his appearance*) Where did you spring from?
Tom Down the motorway from Leeds.
John Are you—er—staying?
Tom In and out, sort of.

There is an awkwardness between them suggesting they did not last part on good terms

Didn't Mum tell you I was coming today?
John She must have forgotten. She has to keep all those orders in her head—a dozen Napolitanas, two dozen Ave Marias.
Tom She said the business is going very well.
John Yes.
Tom Going dancing?
John No. An evening of British catering. We'll be home early. Your—er—tour go well?
Tom Terrific. They tore the place apart at Keighley.
John That must have been an improvement.
Tom I left the van open. I'd better get the rest of my stuff.

Tom goes out

John goes to the drinks-cabinet

Helen comes in looking angry

John Did you find it?
Helen No.
John I told you. It's gone. (*He gestures at Tom's guitar-case*) You forgot to tell me Tom was coming. You're in for a surprise when you see him.
Helen Why?
John Wait and see.
Helen We've got to try and borrow a black tie.

Tom can be seen in the hall, putting down the electronic unit for his guitar. He comes in

Tom!

They kiss. She takes in his appearance

Your hair. What's happened to it?
Tom It's grown a bit, that's all.
Helen What's happened to the leather gear?
Tom Some kid's probably wearing it in Zimbabwe. I gave it to Oxfam. The band split up in Huddersfield.
Helen (*surprised*) When did that happen?
Tom End of last month.
Helen What have you been doing since?
Tom Rehearsing mostly. With another band. We're trying something new. It's pretty original. (*Looking at Helen's outfit*) That's cool.
Helen Thanks. I'm sorry we have to go out tonight, but it's work, not pleasure. You didn't take his black tie, did you?
Tom We don't play funerals.
Helen You don't have one, do you?
Tom Yeah. Polka-dots—that light up.
John Great! I'll go as Elton John.
Helen (*inspiration*) Arthur! He may have one. Phone him.

John makes no move to phone him. Helen gives him a look, goes to the phone herself, and dials

John (*to Tom*) Do you want a drink?
Tom You got any orange juice?
John In the fridge.

Tom goes out into the kitchen

Helen (*into the phone*) Hello, Gwen. Helen. Silly request, but John's lost his black bow-tie. Has Arthur got one? ... OK. (*She looks at her watch*) We'll have to leave in a few minutes. Thanks. (*She puts the phone down*)

Tom comes out of the kitchen with a glass of orange juice

Act I, Scene 4

Tom Any luck?

Helen Arthur's bringing one round.

Tom (*gesturing at John's shoes*) If he hasn't got one, you'll have to use a shoe-lace. Look very Country and Western.

Helen Are you going out tonight?

Tom Yeah. Rehearsing. We're trying to get it all together for next week. We've got some engagements. In the sticks, but it's a start. You know, with new guys it takes time. Don't wait up.

Helen We'll be back late.

Tom Dad said you'd be back early.

Helen looks at John

Either way I've got my key. I'll go up and sort my gear.

He finishes his juice and goes out

Helen looks for her drink, finds the glass—it's empty

John I think I preferred him in his Gestapo phase.

Helen Never happy, are you? You haven't been happy about him since he was fourteen and discovered music.

John Music? He's never discovered music. Just a beat—and dressing-up, of course.

Helen, who has heard it all before, looks at her watch

Helen Where the hell's Arthur?

John You know what really worries me about him?

Helen About Arthur?

John About Tom.

Helen (*wearily*) Yes, I know what worries you about Tom. But tell me again so we can have a fun evening. Get it off your chest.

John No, no. Forget it. All will be joy at the Caterers' Ball.

Helen (*almost a recitation*) He doesn't like anything you like so there must be something wrong with him. He never liked jazz, or games, or drink.

John I haven't said a word.

Helen He's been home five minutes, and already you're starting on him. Whatever he's going to do, our interfering won't help.

John Interfering? I haven't seen him for four months.

Helen (*looking at her watch*) Damn it, where's Arthur? Val will be here in a minute.

John (*reacting as though stung*) Val?

Helen She's picking us up.

John You saved that surprise for the end.

Helen It's pointless taking two cars. You're going to have to sit with her at dinner and be pleasant. You might as well start practising in the car.

John You mean I've got you both for the Caterers' Ball?

Helen She's bringing somebody. David—er—David somebody. He's an architect.

John I'm amazed.

Helen And what does that mean?

John Nothing.

Helen (*getting angry*) Oh, go on. Now you've had a go at Tom, have a go at Val.

He remains irritatingly silent. She gets angrier

She's my partner, and we're starting to make a profit. That's what really threatens you. Having a go at Val is just your way of having a go at me, isn't it?

John You mean I'm transferring my aggressions, Doctor?

Helen When you can't face the truth you always make a joke.

John Isn't that the nature of jokes?

Helen Or a cop-out.

John Or a way of coping.

Helen Well, it hasn't helped you cope. You've never adjusted to my working, and being successful at it. God, when I think of all those professional dinners of yours I had to go to. All your boring colleagues I had to listen to. Now it's your turn, and you don't like it. I sometimes think half the things you've done recently are to get even with me.

John (*suspiciously*) Half of what things?

Helen Do you mind if we don't talk about it now?

John What things? Being unemployed?

Helen I didn't mean *that*.

John Ah!

Helen But if you insist—since you haven't been working you can be bloody unbearable and have a perfect excuse.

John That's right. It's probably the latest plea in wife-battering cases. Sorry, Your Honour, but I'm on the dole.

Helen I think you'd feel a lot better sometimes if you did take a swing at me.

John You never stand still for long enough.

There is a muted sound of a car, and a horn is honked outside. Helen glances out of the window

Helen That's Val. I'm not going to ask her in so you can ruin the evening before it starts. (*She picks up her evening-coat from a chair*) You didn't want to come from the start. Right, don't bother.

John No tie. No Arthur. Can't come.

Helen It's nothing to do with the bloody tie, and you know it. Don't wait up. I mightn't be back.

Helen storms out, banging the door behind her. The front door slams

John goes over to the hi-fi, and puts on a record. It is an Oscar Peterson, fast and jazzy, "You Stepped Out Of A Dream". He flicks his fingers while he lets the music get to him. He goes over to the desk the phone is on, and sits down. Using the desk as an imaginary piano, he starts to play, slowly at first, and then psyching himself up to the full jazz-pianist act, foot thumping, grunts and all

The door opens, and Tom comes in

Act I, Scene 4

Tom Hey!

John, embarrassed, goes over and turns the record down

Still into that old piano stuff?
John I'm a late developer. (*He drinks*)

Tom looks at him, an element of concern for a moment

Tom Are you all right?
John Fine.
Tom Mum told me about what happened. About losing the job.
John Ah!
Tom Got anything else lined up?
John Yes. A couple of things. Nothing definite.
Tom At least the old pizza-factory's still going strong.
John Yes.
Tom Something's bound to turn up.
John Sure. Yes. Bound to.

A silence. Tom picks up his guitar-case

Tom I'm going to be late. See you.
John Yeah.

Tom goes out, leaving the door open

John goes back to the hi-fi, and turns it up to prevent gloom descending

Arthur, let in by Tom, comes in to the living-room

Arthur John!

John turns the hi-fi down

Glad I'm not too late. I had to hunt everywhere for the damn thing. What's happened to Tom?
John In what way?
Arthur He let me in. Where's all his punk gear gone?
John Zimbabwe, I gather.
Arthur What?
John He's in a new phase.
Arthur Helen still getting ready? Take a bloody age, don't they? You should try my Gwen. Sometimes I wait so long I think she's making the damn dress.
John A drink?
Arthur OK. A very quick one. Scotch. Got to get back for supper. (*Inquisitive, he looks at the maps and charts on John's desk*)

John goes and pours a scotch

Any developments yet—jobwise?
John A couple of possibilities. Nothing definite. (*He hands Arthur his drink*)
Arthur You've got to be patient these days to find the right thing. Cheers. (*He drinks*) No good panicking, rushing into the wrong thing.

John Quite.

Arthur I mean fortunately you don't have to, do you?

John No.

Arthur Mind you, if you were a first-class plasterer or plumber I could use you...

John I'm pretty good with pipes. (*During the following, he pours himself another drink, feeling no pain*)

Arthur (*laughing*) I remember what you did to your shower. You know, it's bloody amazing—all this unemployment, but you try to find a really skilled man in the building trades. They're either working on their own and taking it in cash, or else they've pissed off to Australia. Sometimes I feel half the decent people have hopped it.

John I haven't noticed less people on the streets.

Arthur That's because they've let all those other buggers in.

John (*angrily*) Don't start on all that again, please.

Arthur I don't think Gwen wants you to find another job.

John Oh?

Arthur She says it's nice having someone next door she can have coffee with again.

John Ah!

Arthur You'd better watch it.

John reacts

She's thinking about going jogging with you. (*He finishes his drink*) Bit short of stamina, but she'll give you a run for your money. (*He puts his glass down and heads towards the door. Gesturing at John's dinner-jacket*) Oh, I nearly forgot. (*He fishes his bow-tie out of his jacket-pocket, and holds it out to John*)

John pulls his own bow-tie out of his jacket-pocket, and holds it up

John Snap!

Arthur Oh, you found it. Just as well I didn't have to come far. Have fun! Well, thanks for the drink. Anytime you want to wear two bow-ties, give us a shout.

Arthur goes out

John watches him go. He shoves the bow-tie back in his pocket, but the end of it hangs out. He turns up the sound on the hi-fi (Oscar Peterson playing "Watch What Happens"), and then settles down with the jazz, a drink, and the Bible

CURTAIN

ACT II

Scene 1

The same. A few weeks later. Morning

The Baileys' living-room is considerably messier than when we last saw it. The most striking feature of this is the gaping hole in the wall where the second, dining-area, fireplace was. The fireplace and its surround have been removed, and the void in the wall is surrounded by jagged bricks and crumbling plaster. There is a small pile of rubble in front of the hole, most of it having been already cleared. A large dust sheet is spread in front of this area. The furniture has all been pushed up into the living-room area. The sofa and chairs are covered with dust-sheets. There is a Hoover by the kitchen door

When the Curtain *rises John is crouching by the fireplace, sweeping dust into a bucket. He wears very dirty old trousers, a torn tennis shirt, and a pair of grubby tennis-shoes. He starts to brush the last small pile of dust into the bucket. Thoughtfully he takes a small handful and Job-like, throws it up in the air over his head*

Through the open living-room door Tom can be seen coming into the hall. He carries his guitar-case and a small suitcase. He puts them down in the hall, and comes into the living-room. Tom is dressed in his faded pink jeans and a brightly-coloured, light, V-neck sweater. He has a gold chain round his neck. His face bears the slightest remains of make-up, especially round the eyes. He looks very cool and relaxed, his manner and movements those of the happy pot-smoker. He takes in the absent fireplace with a look of amazement

Tom Wow, you've finished it.

John lets his handful of dust run back into the bucket

John Just about. (*Glancing up at Tom, suspicious*) You're up early.
Tom No. Just come in. We played till three, and then had to unwind. We had quite a party.

John hides his disapproval by continuing to fill the bucket till it is full, and the pile of rubble gone. Tom comes over to look at the hole

    It'll be easy for Santa Claus this year.
John Have you had breakfast?
Tom I had supper about an hour ago. (*Peering at the hole and wall*) Is it going to be all right?
John What do you mean?

Tom Am I going to be safe upstairs?
John It's not a structural fireplace. The house won't fall down on you — unless there's a high wind.
Tom What are you going to do with it now?
John Fill it in.
Tom How?
John Bricks and plaster. Unless you've got some other suggestion.
Tom You could ask Arthur to send someone in.
John (*fiercely*) I'm going to do it myself. (*He looks at Tom's face for an instant*) What's wrong with your face?
Tom (*feigning surprise*) In what way — wrong?
John (*with distaste*) Your cheeks.

Tom rubs at his cheeks and looks at his hands

Tom Oh that. It's make-up. From last night's gig.
John I thought you were playing in a pub. You don't wear make-up for that, do you?
Tom No, last night we were on a stage with proper lighting. We all wear some make-up.

John sniffs the air

John You've been smoking pot.
Tom Just a couple. At the party.
John You shouldn't smoke that stuff, and then drive.
Tom I didn't smoke enough to fly home.
John Very funny.

John sets his jaw, takes his brush and full bucket, and goes out into the kitchen

Tom goes towards the living-room door. The phone rings. He comes back to answer it

Tom (*into the phone*) Hello. ... Yes. Who's speaking? ... Hang on a sec. I'll get him. (*He goes towards the kitchen. Calling out*) Dad. Phone.

John comes back into the living-room

Mr Goodison. Executive Manpower.

John goes to the phone

Tom goes into the kitchen

John (*into the phone*) Hello ... fine. ... Who are they? ... Manganese. I don't know anything about manganese. ... It's OK. I'll look it up in an encyclopaedia ...

Tom comes out of the kitchen with a glass of orange juice

... well, I suppose the climate's better than Liverpool. Have you heard anything from Grayling's? ... (*He nods his head glumly*) OK. OK. I can guess the rest. ... (*He writes down a phone number. Wearily*) All right. I'll

Act II, Scene 1

phone and make an appointment. ... Thanks. ... Oh yes, my pecker's right up. (*He puts down the phone*)
Tom (*in a Scouse accent*) Where's better than Liverpool?
John Lusaka.
Tom Where's that?
John The other side of Reading.
Tom It's in Africa somewhere, isn't it?
John Zambia. (*He goes back to the hole in the wall*)

Mary comes in

Mary Good-morning, Tom.
Tom Morning.

Mary looks at John, and his hole, and shakes her head

Mary Oh dear. Whatever will Helen say when she gets back?
John (*raising his voice*) She's always wanted this fireplace out.
Tom (*to Mary*) It lets more air into the room.
Mary (*to John*) At least you'll stop banging now. (*To Tom*) I'm surprised the neighbours didn't complain. He started at seven this morning.
John I didn't sleep very well.
Mary I'm not surprised with all that banging.

Mary suddenly looks vague and lost. John and Tom look at her, concerned for a moment

(*Recovering*) Where's Helen?
John She's still away.
Mary Ah!
Tom Want some shopping today? I'm going out later.
Mary No, thanks. John did it yesterday. Where's Helen?
John (*a beat*) Reading.
Tom (*quietly*) Zambia.

Mary glances at Tom suspiciously as though she caught his remark

Mary She didn't tell me she was going anywhere for so long.
John She's trying to extend the business in the Home Counties. Looking for new outlets.
Mary (*to Tom*) Are you going to work?
Tom I've just been to work.

That confuses her. She looks at her watch

I'm working nights.

Mary looks at the absent fireplace again

Mary Why did you take that out?
John (*wearily*) Because it was there.
Mary Weren't you going to work this week?
John No. Not this week.
Mary Ah! I came in to ask for something. What was it?

Tom Not shopping.
Mary No.
Tom Dad's wallpapering.

She thinks hard

Mary Yes. That's it. It's peeling in the corners.
John You've told me already.
Mary It's no good having wallpaper in a kitchen. It's the steam.
John Maybe you shouldn't boil anything for a day or two.
Mary How do I make tea then?
John I'll put some more paste on later.
Mary You should have let Mr Hollis do it. (*She nods at the hole in the wall*) And that.

Mary turns and goes out, shutting the door. There is the sound of her door shutting in the hall

Tom finishes his orange juice

Tom How long are you going to keep that up?
John What?
Tom Telling her you've got a job, and that Mum's coming back.

John is silent. He unwinds the Hoover flex

I had lunch with Mum yesterday.
John What did she tell you?
Tom That she'd come back from that dinner. You were asleep, and the bow-tie was hanging out of your pocket, where you had it all along. You should have buried it in the garden.
John People don't leave each other over hidden bow-ties.
Tom She said that was the final straw. That's how you've been all along about her work.
John Now you've got her side of the story.
Tom She didn't say any more than that.
John Is she still staying with Val?
Tom Yes.
John (*sourly*) I knew Val would be supportive.
Tom She said financially it was the only alternative, unless you wanted to stay with Val.

John gives a sour smile

John Did she say who gets her mother?
Tom No, but she said if you weren't going to tell her what's happened, she would.
John Fine. (*He plugs in the Hoover*)
Tom I suppose I should contribute to the housekeeping while I'm staying.
John Just buy your own orange juice.
Tom OK. I'm going to bed.

As Tom turns to go there is a banging on the front window. Tom looks out the window

Act II, Scene 1   41

It's Gwen. I'll let her in.

Tom goes out, taking his guitar-case and suitcase

John looks embarrassed. There is the sound of the front door opening and Tom and Gwen exchanging greetings

(*Off*) I've been to work. I'm just going to bed. Good-night.

Gwen appears in the living-room doorway. Tom goes across the hall, and up the stairs

Gwen (*calling after Tom*) Good-night. (*She comes into the living-room. She wears a pastel-coloured tracksuit, and matching jogging-shoes. To John*) He works funny hours, doesn't he?
John Yes.

Gwen notices the hole in the wall

Gwen God, you've actually got it out.
John Yes. I got carried away yesterday.
Gwen What are you going to do now?
John You're the third person who's asked that this morning.
Gwen You're going to fill it in?
John It's that, or ask Arthur.
Gwen (*worriedly*) You can't ask him.
John Why not?
Gwen (*slightly embarrassed*) If you have his men working here ...
John It's OK. I'll finish it myself.
Gwen Have you heard anything from Helen yet?
John Yes. She finally phoned this morning—about some financial matters.
Gwen (*worriedly*) You don't think she suspects—about us, do you?
John I can't see how.
Gwen I feel dreadful suddenly—sort of guilty.
John Why? Did you feel less guilty when she was around?
Gwen (*contemplating*) Yes and no. It's funny. I can't work it out. (*Pause*) Aren't you going jogging this morning?
John My back isn't too good—(*gesturing at the hole in the wall*) after that. Not to mention my legs, lungs ... You go.
Gwen I don't want to run on my own.
John (*mock-seriously*) Sooner or later we all have to run on our own.
Gwen Very profound this morning, aren't we? I'll make some coffee.

She goes into the kitchen

He looks after her, as though anxious to be rid of her. He switches on the Hoover and starts to hoover up the dust and debris on the dust-sheet in front of the fireplace. The Hoover makes that crackling noise of hard bits and pieces going into the works. It splutters into silence

John Oh, shit! (*He gets down on the floor, upturns the Hoover, and starts prodding around inside*)

Gwen comes out of the kitchen with two mugs of coffee

Gwen You're not meant to suck that stuff into a Hoover. (*She takes the mugs over to a coffee-table, puts them down, and takes the dust-cover off the sofa*) Try emptying the bag.

He struggles, bad-temperedly, to undo the Hoover and get the bag out, but doesn't know how to do it

(*Coming over to him*) Let me do it.

John (*irritably*) I can do it. I'll do it later. (*He bangs the Hoover down and goes over to the coffee. He picks up a mug, takes a mouthful, and pulls a face*) You've put sugar in it.

Gwen That's mine. The other one's yours.

He changes mugs and sits down

Gwen goes over to the Hoover, instantly finds the catch, opens it and takes out the bag. She takes it out into the kitchen

(*Off*) Where are the Hoover bags?

John I've told you. I'll do it later.

Gwen comes back

Gwen Do you think she's going to come back?

John I don't know.

Gwen Is she still staying with Val?

John Yes.

Gwen (*shaking her head*) It's weird. I feel, you know, sort of ...

John Don't.

Gwen What?

John Feel responsible. I've told you, it's nothing to do with you.

Gwen (*almost offended*) Oh!

John Unless of course, you want to feel responsible. If that makes you feel better ...

Gwen That's a rotten thing to say. (*She scowls at him*)

John I'm in a rotten mood.

Gwen You've heard about that Liverpool job, haven't you?

He nods

You didn't want it anyway, did you? (*She takes his arm*) Something will turn up. Don't get depresed again.

John (*with a false smile*) Me? Depressed? I'm getting to like being unemployed. Oh, at first you feel a bit low, but then you get quite used to it. I mean it's got its consolations, hasn't it? Love on the dole, knocking down walls. No stress of earning a living. In fact having to go back to work would be an intrusion. I'd resent it.

Gwen Well come on, love, something will turn up when you least expect it.

John Oh, yes.

Gwen Don't give up. Arthur says that's half the trouble these days.

John What is?

Gwen Too many people have given up. He's always saying nobody here wants to work.

John Everybody except honest, white Arthur.

Act II, Scene 1   43

Gwen You really don't like Arthur, do you?
John You mean, as you like Helen, I should like Arthur?
Gwen No. I didn't mean that.
John Does it matter?
Gwen No.

Silence. She starts to go

Well, if we're not going jogging, I'd better get back to my chores. You'd better get back to your wall.

He takes her hand, stopping her going

John I'm sorry. Things have just got me down this morning.
Gwen Don't pull everybody down with you.
John I'm sorry.
Gwen It's OK. I know how you feel. I've been stuck at home for years.
John At least you've learned how to empty a Hoover.

She leans affectionately against him

Gwen It took me ages.
John I didn't mean to snap at you.
Gwen Arthur went this morning.

John pulls away from her, horrified

John What? He's left?
Gwen Only for the night. For that meeting in Birmingham.
John (*relieved*) Oh! Oh yes.
Gwen (*taking his arm affectionately*) We could go out to dinner for once. (*Registering his lack of enthusiasm*) It might cheer you up.
John Yes.
Gwen You don't want to, do you?
John (*feigning enthusiasm*) No. No. Of course I do. But it'll have to be somewhere cheap and ethnic.
Gwen No. I want to go somewhere grand and expensive. I've got a new dress I want to wear. And I'm going to pay.
John All right. I'll wear my interview suit, and look six months younger.
Gwen You don't mind?
John Mind?
Gwen I thought you might be ... old-fashioned. You once said something about pimping ...
John This isn't off immoral earnings. After all, you are married to Arthur.
Gwen And he owes you a dinner. (*She kisses him*)

There is the sound of the front door opening and closing. Gwen pulls away quickly from John

Helen comes in. She registers Gwen in her tracksuit first, and then takes in John

Neither look comfortable with the situation. Helen doesn't at first see the demolished wall

Helen Hello.
Gwen Hello, Helen. Just came in to drag your hubby out jogging.
Helen (*to Gwen*) I came back to see how everything was. (*To John*) Why are you covered in dust?
John *Voilà.*
Helen My God, you've done it.
John Now tell me you wanted to keep the fireplace.
Helen No. It's a wonderful hole. What got into you?
John You know—between jobs.
Helen Do you know how to fill it in?
John No, but I'm going to go to evening classes.
Helen (*to Gwen*) How's Arthur?
Gwen Fine.
Helen Not jogging too, is he?
Gwen Not Arthur. Jogging is John's idea. Business still going well?
Helen Yes. If you two were going jogging don't let me stop you. I'm going in to see Mum.
Gwen No, John's had his exercise for the day—on that wall. I'd better go before I go off the idea. I'll—er—see you around.
Helen Yes, 'bye.

Gwen goes

John She's been very helpful—does Mary's shopping some mornings.
Helen I'm glad she's being such a good neighbour. So you're managing all right?
John I'm managing.
Helen Any developments on the job front?
John Nothing definite. I may just work for the Council. It'll be autumn soon. I'll do the leaves. Just my luck they won't fall this year. Did you come for your spare toothbrush?
Helen No. I'm OK for toothbrushes. I think I'll go and see how Mum is.
John Why? Do you think I beat her up when you're not here?
Helen Tom said you hadn't told her what's happened.
John What has happened?
Helen We're going our own ways for the time being.
John Women's rights?
Helen Men's rights, too.
John (*angrily*) Big deal. I get Tom, your mother and the dole. You get the pizzas and Val.
Helen I am contributing towards the house.
John Thanks. Half of it is yours anyway.
Helen We both need time to sort things out. I'll get on with my job. You can get on with looking for yours.

Her reasonableness infuriates him

John Oh, very tactful.
Helen Look, at the moment I just need some peace and quiet myself.
John And you get that at Val's.

Helen Yes.
John I hope that's all you get.
Helen God, you've got a nasty mind. When you're down you really lash out, don't you?
John At least I don't kick people when they're down.
Helen No. You kick them regardless. (*Gesturing at the invisible fireplace in the "fourth wall"*) Why don't you take out your aggression on the other fireplace while you're about it?
John (*furiously*) Right. I'll get the hammer.

He storms off and bangs the door

She is about to do the same, then hesitates, before going towards Mary's flat

Then she goes and slams the door

Black-out. Music: "What Is This Thing Called Love"—J. J. Johnson

Scene 2

The same. That night

John comes into the darkened living-room. He switches on the lights from the switches beside the door. An overhead light and a lamp come on. He is dressed in his smart grey interview suit, a blue shirt and colourful tie, and looks very well wined and dined. He surveys the room, and decides the lighting is too bright. He turns off the overhead light, crosses, and puts on another lamp. He goes over to the drinks-cabinet, opens it, and examines the low state of his supplies. He pulls out a bottle of brandy, peers at the level inside, shakes it. There is just enough left at the bottom. He gets out two brandy glasses. He goes to the hi-fi, selects a record and puts on a slow and romantic jazz piano number, Errol Garner's "Summertime". The scene is set. He looks round and shakes his head. It is all too corny, he turns off the music, puts another lamp on, and goes back to the drinks-cabinet

Gwen comes in through the living-room door. She wears a short evening-coat over a pretty dress. She has clearly had plenty to drink at dinner

Gwen I peeped in at the kids. They're both fast asleep.
John Good. (*Lifting up the brandy bottle*) Nightcap? There's just enough left.
Gwen Ooh! Yes, please. (*She takes off her coat and puts it on a chair*)

He pours two glasses of brandy. She comes over and takes one from him

Gwen Cheers.
John Cheers.
Gwen That was a lovely dinner.
John I've never eaten avocados *and* smoked salmon first.
Gwen Very *nouveau riche*. You know, that's the first time I've ever been out to dinner alone—with another man, in ... (*she thinks*) ... twelve years.
John The bill was horrific. You should have let me contribute.

Gwen Why? (*She giggles*) Arthur can put in another bidet for cash. (*She sits on the sofa, kicking her shoes off*) It's nice paying. I like it. Better than the bad old days.

John Which ones?

Gwen When the man paid, and afterwards you worried about what he was going to want to do to get his money's worth. This way I can say no—or yes. (*She holds a hand out to him. Pause*) Put some music on. Something nice and soft.

John Funny you should say that. (*He goes over and puts on the record that is on the turntable. He goes back and sits beside her. He lets his right hand perform a few Errol Garner trills in the air*)

She leans against him

Gwen Did you really play the piano?

John Yes. Played by ear a bit. Then I had lessons for ages.

Gwen And you wanted to play like that?

John I was the wrong colour. Took me ages to realize that though. When I did, I sold the piano, and bought records.

Gwen I wanted to be a tap-dancer. I had lessons. I wasn't good enough either. Why don't you take up the piano again?

John Too old.

Gwen Not too old to dance, are you?

John Absolutely.

Gwen Killjoy. Come on.

She pulls him up and they start to dance together, a slightly jazzed-up quickstep in the empty part of the room in front of the hole in the wall

John Do you come here often?

Gwen Yes. Mostly mornings.

She kisses him playfully, and breaks away from him. She goes into her own improvised steps, showing that once she could really dance. John does little more than accompany her. The number ends. She holds on to him

Funny being here at night.

John Yes.

Gwen We could just go upstairs to bed.

John looks hesitant for an instant

Unless you don't want to.

John No, no. It's your choice. You paid. (*He kisses her on the cheek, and goes and turns off the hi-fi*)

Gwen goes out of the door, and he switches off the lights and follows her

After a moment, the door opens and a figure, which could be Helen but is in fact Tom in drag, comes in. He has long blonde hair and wears a longish dress over black stockings and short boots, and many jangling accessories. He looks like a woman, but not too grotesque. He is just discernible as he crosses and goes into the kitchen

Act II, Scene 2   47

There is the sound of the fridge door opening. The light from the fridge spills out into the kitchen. There is the sound of a glass clinking, something being poured and put back in the fridge. The fridge is shut

Tom comes back into the living-room

The living-room door opens and the light is switched on. Gwen comes in. She is dressed, but looks a bit rumpled, and isn't wearing shoes

She crosses to the chair to collect her coat, handbag and shoes and does not see Tom standing frozen in front of the hole in the wall, clutching a glass of orange juice. Gwen turns, sees this apparition, and screams. Tom drops the glass of orange juice

Tom S-s-sh! It's Tom.

Gwen stares horrified at him

Gwen No! What ...
Tom (*embarrassed*) I thought everyone ... would be asleep.

There is the sound of John pounding down the stairs. He rushes into the room, wearing his dressing-gown over bare legs

John Sssh! (*He shuts the door*) Why the hell are you screaming? (*He sees Tom*) Who are you? (*He stops dead in his tracks, his mouth staying open*)
Gwen It's Tom.

There is a silent, horrified moment

John Good God. (*Looking heavenward*) Oh no!

Tom is the first to recover, though he still has trouble getting words out

Tom (*to John*) I thought you'd be in bed (*glancing at Gwen*)—asleep.
John (*embarrassed now*) Gwen and I were ... We—er—went out to ...

Mary rushes in through the open living-room door. She has a quilted dressing-gown over her nightie, and carries a large brass candlestick at the ready. She stops when she sees the trio confronting each other

Mary Oh! It's you. I thought it was burglars.
John No.
Gwen No. (*Pause*) We were all out having dinner ...
John And came back for a nightcap—(*he is still in shock, and frantic for Mary not to recognize Tom, and explain his own bedtime attire*)—I spilled on my suit, so I had to change. (*Gesturing at Gwen*) You know Gwen, don't you?
Mary Of course. (*She peers suspiciously at Tom*)
John And Gwen's friend, Carol.
Mary Ah! (*Peering at Tom*) We've met, haven't we?
Gwen I'm sorry if we were too noisy.
Mary (*suspiciously*) I thought I heard a scream.
John A scream?
Gwen Oh, that was me. John told a hysterical story.
Mary (*unconvinced*) He did?

Gwen Yes. (*To John*) You must tell it to Mary sometime.
John Yes.
Mary It must have been very funny. (*To Tom*) You dropped your drink. (*She gestures at the spilled glass of orange juice on the floor*)
Tom Oh!
John (*fast*) I'll get a cloth from the kitchen.
Tom (*high-pitched*) No, I will.

Tom goes out into the kitchen

Mary watches suspiciously, trying to remember where she's seen "her" before

Mary I'm going back to bed then.
John Right.
Gwen Good-night.
John Sleep well.
Mary (*looking at them disapprovingly*) Good-night.

Mary goes out

John and Gwen look at each other. John visibly slumps, and shuts his eyes

Gwen I'd better be—er—getting back. (*Indicating upstairs*) I'll get my things ... Thanks for—dinner. I'll see myself out.
John (*nodding*) Thanks.

He starts to go with her to the door. She motions him to stay

Gwen It's all right. I know the way.

She goes out. There is the sound of the front door banging

Tom comes back in with a floor-cloth

John (*goggling at him*) What the hell!

Tom calmly goes and mops up the orange juice

Tom There wasn't anywhere to change after the gig. I thought you'd be fast asleep.
John I wish I had been fast asleep. I wish it was all a dream. This—everything.
Tom There was no need to tell Gran that. She'd have coped.
John Coped? Are you crazy?

Tom straightens up

I can't talk to you in ... You look obscene.

Tom gathering himself, tries to play it cool

Tom Thanks. It went down well at the Club.
John Club? I thought you were playing in pubs.
Tom (*boldly*) No. We're playing the drag clubs in Kent.
John (*really shocked*) In Kent!
Tom Look, I thought you'd be in bed—asleep. I'm sorry you got a shock. Don't jump to any conclusion, that's all.

Act II, Scene 2   49

John (*sarcastically*) Oh, no. I wouldn't do that. (*Anger breaking through*) Really you just want to play scrum-half for the Harlequins. (*Pause*) The other—guys—you play with—are they all ...

Tom In drag? Yes. (*Pause*) I know what you're thinking. It's not as cut and dried as that.

John Terrific.

Tom Anyway, if we are all gay, would that be worse?

John Worse? Worse than what?

Tom (*shrugging*) Sleeping with someone else's wife. I mean, if we're going to be all moral about it, doesn't it say in the Bible—thou shalt not commit adultery? It doesn't say ...

John (*furiously*) It does.

Tom Not in the Ten Commandments.

John All right then. Somewhere else. In Sodom and Gomorrah. They all got turned into pillars of salt. Do you want me to look it up?

Tom If it'll make you feel better.

John (*taking a deep breath*) Do you mind if we don't have a theological discussion while you're wearing a wig?

Tom Sorry. I forgot about it. (*He pulls off the wig*) Better? Anyway, whether you understand it or not, it's a relief to be honest.

John (*acidly*) Oh, good.

Tom At the moment, I'm not definitely one way or the other.

John Ah! Terrific.

Tom I mean you're lucky to know what you like. It's even more convenient if it lives next door.

John You mean I should feel guiltier than you?

Tom Why should anyone feel guilty? Relax.

John (*furiously*) Relax?

Tom You need a drink.

John There isn't any left.

Tom gets a tin out of his pocket, opens it, and pulls out a thin reefer, which he offers to John

Tom Have one of these?

John (*looking at the reefer in horror*) I don't want one of those.

Tom It'll help you relax.

John (*hysteria mounting*) Relax! Oh yes, one must relax. That solves everything these days. The whole bloody world's arse-about-face, but as long as you relax ... what's it matter?

Tom (*putting the reefer away*) That's why people drink, isn't it?

John And take rat-poison, or watch telly all night. Relax. Who cares? I mean why should I worry if I never work again? Relax. I've changed into a housewife. Your mother's turned into a feller who earns the money. You're a don't-know. If you bring home a girl, or a bloke, or a girl who's a bloke, or a bloke who's a girl, I should just relax. I'll go to yoga with Gwen. Sit on the floor with my legs tied in knots, making a high-pitched buzz. (*He slumps down on the chair, shaking his head*) I can't believe this is all happening. Christ, and we're a small family. Can you imagine what's going on out there? (*He gestures wildly at the Great Outside*)

Tom Getting hysterical won't help. You'll have Gran in again.

John She's the only one in the family who's sane. That's because half the time she doesn't know what the fuck's going on.

Tom At least she accepts things. Not you. You want everything to stand still—me, Mum, your job. You never accept anything that doesn't go your way. I remember when I didn't like maths—or the piano—oh boy!

John (*angry again*) That's right. I was a rotten father. I was Hitler, Mussolini . . .

Tom I never said that.

John But it was next on your list. I got it all wrong. I wanted you to grow up to be Albert Einstein, Oscar Peterson, and win Wimbledon. And you just wanted to be Judy Garland.

Tom David Bowie.

John And now I'm being punished for wanting anything at all.

Tom No-one's being punished for anything. It all just happens. You've got to go with it.

John Go with it.

Tom Just go with it. For all we know we may be reincarnated as grasshoppers.

John If I'd known you were going to grow up as a bisexual Hindu . . .

Tom (*irritated*) Whatever I am, I won't be hanging around to embarrass you. We're starting a tour tomorrow. I'm going to bed.

John shuts his eyes, and screws up his face in weariness and frustration

It's all right. I won't kiss you good-night.

Tom goes out

John sits, eyes shut still. Then, as usual, his gloom is dispelled by an attack of the manics. He gets up, throwing his hands in the air, gesturing

John That's it. It all just happens. You've got to go with it. Dream—nightmare, what's it matter? It all just happens. Phut! (*He goes to the bookshelves, takes the framed photographs and starts throwing them*) Wife—son—phut! (*He takes the magazines*—Civil Engineer—*and files on the shelves, and starts throwing them*) Work—job—career—phut! (*The next book on the shelf beside the magazines is the Bible, where he put it back in Act I. He takes it, glancing at the cover*) Oxen—camels—asses—phut! (*He drops the Bible into the wastepaper-basket. He stands utterly beaten, sniffing back tears, and then he looks upwards*) Oh God!

Fade to Black-out

SCENE 3

The same. The next morning.

The Lights come up on the living-room. It is as we left it the night before, except John, still in his dressing-gown, is sprawled-out asleep on the sofa. The Bible is beside him

Mary comes in. She sees him on the sofa, and goes towards him, looking troubled. She registers the Bible beside him. She decides against waking him, and goes out into the kitchen

The sound of Mary rattling about in the kitchen wakes him up. He comes to very slowly. Then, remembering, he groans. He picks up the Bible, and sits up

Mary comes out of the kitchen, carrying a tray with a glass of orange juice, and some cereal and milk on it

John Hello. What time is it?
Mary Half-past nine.
John God, I feel terrible.
Mary You should have gone to bed. I'm making you some breakfast. Have your juice.
John Thanks. I just fell asleep here. I was reading. (*He picks up the Bible, trying to act as naturally as possible in front of Mary*)
Mary The Bible again?

He crosses to the table carrying the Bible

John (*casually*) I was looking something up—couldn't find it, so I thought I'd see how old Job ends up.

Mary looks at him worriedly

Mary You read that before.
John Never finished it. I gave up when the three comforters were droning on about how he should put up with his miserable lot.
Mary Well, he did, didn't he?
John More or less, but you won't believe this. It's got a happy ending. I skipped to the last two pages. The Lord changed his fortunes, and gave him twice as much as before. Everyone came and gave him money. (*He drinks his orange juice. Again, he covers his misery with a manic quality. He taps the pages of the Bible, reading selectively from it*)

Mary looks at him as though he has taken one of his turns again

The Lord blessed the latter end of Job more than his beginning ... fourteen thousand sheep, six thousand camels, a thousand yoke of oxen, a thousand she-asses, plus seven sons and three daughters. No mention of his wife though ... (*his eye scans on*) ... and he lived to be a hundred and forty. How about that? A hundred and forty.
Mary Yes, dear. Well in those days a year probably wasn't as long. I'll get your toast. The kettle's on. Tea or coffee?
John Coffee. There's instant there.

Mary goes out

The minute she is out of the door, John's act crumbles. He is back in the deep dumps. He pushes the Bible away, and finishes his orange juice

Mary comes out of the kitchen with a round of toast, and a mug of coffee. She puts it down in front of him

Thanks.

There is a silence, while he butters the toast, and she watches him

(*A big effort*) Sorry about disturbing you last night. I shouldn't have brought them back here for a nightcap. We'd all had a bit too much to drink—celebrating. It was Gwen's friend's birthday. Arthur was away so Gwen roped me in.

Mary nods and turns away. John, relieved, goes back to his toast. Mary turns back to him

Mary You shouldn't fight with Tom. He's a good boy at heart.
John (*getting the toast down*) When was I fighting with Tom?
Mary Don't be daft. I'm not blind—or deaf. You shouldn't worry about him. A lot of them are like that these days.
John A lot of *whom* are like *what*?
Mary Young people in those groups. Gender benders. They dress up. I've seen them on television. They're not really, you know, bi—trans— whatever it is.
John (*drily*) You know all about that, do you?
Mary You can't not know about those things these days. Even if you don't want to.
John I suppose they phone in to ask whether they're boys or girls.
Mary You hear some funny things on those late-night programmes. Makes you realize how lucky you are.
John I should start listening to them.
Mary I suppose it all went on in my day too. We just didn't hear about it on the wireless. Nothing's really new. (*Looking at him closely*) We had unemployment as well. It was up North then too. You're not unique.
John You've known?
Mary I know plenty about the dole too.
John Know a lot, don't you?
Mary Two years after we were married Jack was out of work for ages. I wish I'd had a job and could have supported him till he found another. I couldn't have gone into business like Helen. Women didn't in those days. So some things have changed for the better.
John (*morosely*) For women. And the other lot.
Mary Poor old Jack. As soon as he got started again the War came along and took him off. Afterwards he never got back to what he was. (*She sits down, a little tearful*) I think it was the worry about it all that gave him a bad heart. I often think if I could have helped him more ... He was like you. Had to do everything himself. Didn't want a helping hand with anyone.
John We're probably all living in the Book of Job.
Mary Oh, I know you're turning to religion. It's a comfort to some, but I don't believe in it. At least when you phone in on one of those programmes you get a straight answer. (*She stands up, returning to*

Act II, Scene 3   53

practical matters) You should have a wash and a shave. You'd feel better. Now there was something important I was going to ask you. What was it?
John About Tom? Helen? My next job?
Mary (*ignoring these suggestions*) My wallpaper. You're going to put some more paste on my wallpaper today, aren't you?
John (*wearily*) No, not today. I'll do it tomorrow.
Mary You said that yesterday. And the day before.
John Please. Tomorrow.
Mary They didn't used to say *that* in *this* country.

Mary goes out

John despondently finishes his toast and coffee

Tom comes in through the open living-room door. For the first time he is dressed in what used to pass as normal clothes; a tweed sports jacket, grey trousers, a white shirt and striped tie. He looks suddenly very young and clean-cut—a Public School prefect

John has his back to him, and doesn't hear him come in

Tom Morning, Dad.

John turns round slowly and then goggles at him

I'm just off.
John What are you meant to be this morning?
Tom I thought it would make you feel better. I wore it at speech-day. The year I left school.
John Will your group talk to you?
Tom (*shrugging*) They'll think I'm a bit kinky, but what the hell?
John Have you had any breakfast?
Tom While you were asleep. You looked zonked.
John (*embarrassed*) I read for a bit, and must have fallen asleep on the sofa.
Tom The Bible. I saw. Not going to be born again are you?
John No. Once was enough. Where are you playing?
Tom We've got some dates on the South Coast. Resorts mainly. (*Pause*) I hope something good comes up for you soon. I mean I hope you don't have to go to Zambia.
John So do I.

The doorbell rings

Tom I'll get it. 'Bye now.
John (*quietly*) 'Bye, Tom.

Tom goes

There is the sound of Tom's and Gwen's voices exchanging "hellos" and "goodbyes". John stands still in the middle of the room

Gwen comes in. She is very smartly dressed, in a businesslike way

Gwen He's a bit of a quick change artist, isn't he? (*She looks at him*) Are you all right?

John I've managed to keep breakfast down — so far.

Gwen Christ, I got a shock last night. Did you know he ... (*She can't find the words*)

John (*vehemently*) No, I didn't. (*Almost to himself*) I suppose that just leaves boils.

Gwen (*hearing him, concerned*) You haven't got boils, have you? You didn't have them last night.

John No, but I mean that's bound to be next, isn't it? Or I'll be visited by three comforters from the Inland Revenue.

She looks at him worriedly

Gwen Did you sleep at all last night?

The phone rings

John That's probably Helen to say she's going to marry Val, and would Tom be a bridesmaid.

Gwen I'll make some coffee.

He answers the phone

Gwen goes out into the kitchen

John (*into the phone*) Hello.... Oh, hello, Mr Goodison.... Yes, I did go to the final interview. I told them I'd think about going to Lusaka. ... (*Weary and desperate*) They really want me, do they? ... Yes, I've thought about it ... it was inevitable. It's boils. Finally it's boils.... No, no, just a figure of speech.... Yes, I'll go.... No, I shan't be taking my family.... Yes, I'm fine. Been a difficult decision, that's all. ... At least this way you'll be able to cross me off your books finally. ... Right, I will. ... You've been very kind. 'Bye. (*He puts the phone down*)

Gwen comes out of the kitchen with two mugs of coffee

Gwen Not bad news?

John No, no. Good old Goodison. He really cares about the unemployed. Poor, compassionate, old sod.

He takes his coffee and goes and sits down, dejected. He takes in Gwen's appearance for the first time

Gwen Wait till you hear my news. I've got an interview for a job.

John (*staggered*) What?

Gwen I answered an ad. last week. I didn't want to say anything in case it came to nothing.

John For what?

Gwen An advertising agency. They do market research. They want a part-timer.

John (*sourly*) Great. Arthur'll be delighted.

Gwen That was all talk. Wait till he comes home and finds his dinner isn't ready, or he has to do the shopping at the weekend. Anyway I'm not going to tell him till I've got it. (*She comes over and sits beside him. She strokes his hair*) Remember what you said?

Act II, Scene 3   55

John No. I never do.
Gwen Everybody has to run on their own sometime. (*She kisses his cheek*) Anyway it's only part-time. I'll need to earn some money if we're going to go on eating-out.

The doorbell rings

John (*getting up*) And to lend me for the milkman. I haven't paid him for a month, and he rings every bloody morning now.

John goes out. There is sound of his voice exchanging greetings with Arthur at the front door

Arthur (*off*) Is Gwen here?
John (*off*) Yes. Inside.

Arthur comes in wearing a sports jacket and open-necked shirt, followed by an uneasy-looking John

Arthur Found an empty house next door. Thought she might have come in for elevenses.

Gwen and John are both thrown by Arthur's unexpected arrival. Not knowing what to expect, they try very hard to act naturally, but it is only a light cover for their apprehensiveness

Gwen Oh, I thought ... (*adjusting her strangulated tone*) ... you were going straight into the office.
Arthur No. Had a dreadful drive down from B'rum. Two pile-ups on the M1. Going to put my feet up for the rest of the morning. So I'll be in for lunch.
Gwen Ah!

Arthur smiles at John. It could be a friendly smile—glad to see my wife and my friend getting on so well. Or it could be a devious smile, as Arthur waits for his moment

John Want a coffee, Arthur?
Arthur No, thanks. Need something a bit stronger after that drive.
John Yes, well ... (*Going to the drinks-cabinet*) I'm a bit low on the hard stuff after last night.
Arthur Had a party last night, did you?

Gwen shoots John a fierce warning look

John No, no. Just—er—Tom was home late and—er—Mary, my mother-in-law came in ... and she ... (*He fiddles nervously among the empty bottles in the drinks-cabinet. He comes up with the remains of a bottle of sherry*) No scotch, I'm afraid. There's some sherry. Will that do?
Arthur Yes. OK.
Gwen Fine. Good meeting in Birmingham?
Arthur Load of bloody twisters. (*He looks at her closely*) Bit dressed up for coffee aren't you?
Gwen I was ... er ... going out for lunch with ... Jean.

Arthur Jean?
Gwen Jean Byers.
Arthur (*suspiciously*) I thought you didn't see her anymore.

John brings over Arthur's drink

Gwen She called while you were away—to be friendly.
Arthur Ah! (*Taking the drink*) Thanks. Cheers. (*He takes a big swig, almost finishing it. He turns and sees the hole in the wall*) Bloody hell! You've done it yourself.
John Yes, well—passes the time, you know.
Arthur You going to fill it in too?
John Thought I'd try.
Arthur As there's a chimney there, you know you're going to have to cap the chimney stack, or put a ventilator in.
John Thanks. I hadn't thought of that.
Arthur You'll get damp in the wall otherwise.

Gwen looks apprehensively at Arthur. Is he just sparring?

Gwen I'm going to be late for my—er—lunch. (*She gets up. To Arthur*) There's plenty of stuff in the fridge. I'll see you later, Arthur. 'Bye John. Thanks for coffee.
John Have a good—lunch.

Gwen goes

There is a moment's silence between Arthur and John

Arthur You've—er—been seeing quite a bit of Gwen recently, haven't you?
John She pops in sometimes for coffee. Even been jogging with me a couple of times.
Arthur Yes, she said. (*Pause*) You find her all right?
John Yes. I find her all right.
Arthur Not—er—acting differently—strangely?
John No.
Arthur I've been worried about her recently. She seems sort of moody, preoccupied round the house.
John Oh?
Arthur Not like her old self. More rows, you know. But she doesn't get over them like she used to. She's got quite aggressive.
John I haven't noticed anything.
Arthur Pretty odd her going off all dressed up like that to see someone she never sees.
John But that friend phoned her, didn't she?
Arthur Say it wasn't an old friend? I mean, I wouldn't know, would I? She could be meeting someone—regularly.
John Oh!
Arthur No. I'm sure not. Not Gwen.
John No.
Arthur Maybe she just needs to get out more. Perhaps do some job. She's a bright girl, really. She could find a job easily.

Act II, Scene 4

John Oh! I'm sure she could.
Arthur It would help me too. Business isn't great at the moment. What with that, and Gwen's moods, I haven't been feeling so great myself recently.
John Ah! I'm sorry.
Arthur I didn't mean to rabbit on. It's just in my work you don't get much chance to talk to anybody. (*Perking up*) Hey, maybe that's the answer. I send Gwen out to work, and stay at home like you. Then I can come in here for coffee instead of her. We can talk, go jogging. Lunchtime, nip down to the boozer, spot of darts. Then over to the betting shop, a little flutter—life of Riley.
John Terrific.

There is an off-stage thump from the direction of the hall

Arthur What's that?
John Must be the milkman. When his hands are full, he thumps.

John goes out. There is the sound of him opening and closing the front door. He comes back into the room

Nobody there.

Across the hall Mary's door opens slightly

Mary (*off, faint but close*) John! John!
John Oh God! It's Mary.

John turns and rushes out. Arthur goes after him. They go in through Mary's door

After a moment or two, Arthur, looking desperate, rushes back into the living-room

He grabs the phone directory. Frantic, he looks up a number, and then dials

Arthur (*into the phone*) Hello. ... Ambulance ... (*He hangs on a second*) Come on ... Hello, yes. Can you get an ambulance over here quickly? Forsythe Road. There's been an accident. An old lady. She fell. In her kitchen. ... (*Impatiently*) Does it matter where? Will you send a bloody ambulance. ... Mrs Mary Ferguson. Seventeen Forsythe Road ...

The Lights fade as the sound of an ambulance siren swells up and then goes into music: "My Funny Valentine" (J. J. Johnson and Stan Getz)

Scene 4

The same. A couple of weeks later. Morning

When the Lights come up there are two changes to the set. The hole in the wall has been plastered up, except for an uneven gap left for a ventilator and the desk and chair are back in their usual positions

There is the sound of the front door opening and closing

Helen comes in, dressed in her normal style for a working-day. She has her usual big sling-bag over her shoulder, and in her other hand she carries a plastic shopping-bag that contains a box

John comes out of the kitchen with plaster and trowel

John Oh, it's you.
Helen Yes. Has somebody else got a front-door key? (*She puts the plastic bag down carefully on a chair*)
John I thought you said after I'd pushed your mother off a ladder you weren't going to speak to me anymore.
Helen I didn't say that. I said if you'd done her damned wallpaper when she'd asked, she wouldn't have needed to go up a ladder.
John I told you I did her wallpaper. If she wasn't boiling kettles all the time, like some demented midwife, it wouldn't have started coming down again. Anyway I've done it again, and hidden all the ladders. If she decides to repair the roof it's not my responsibility.
Helen (*looking at the wall*) You've filled it in.
John Yes. (*Pause*) Got to put in a ventilator, of course, as there's a chimney there. Otherwise you get damp in the wall. Easier than capping a chimney.
Helen (*warmer*) Getting quite handy in your old age, aren't you?
John I thought I'd try embroidery next. (*He goes back to his sweeping-up*) Of course, it's still half your house, so if you don't want a ventilator I'll leave it, and you can climb up and cap the chimney.
Helen A ventilator will be fine.

He starts to fold the dustsheet

Heard any more about a job?
John Yes.

A silence. He isn't volunteering any more

Helen Tom mentioned you were considering a job in Zambia.
John Yes.
Helen You're not serious about going there, are you?
John We're discussing final terms.

Helen is shocked, but doesn't want it to show. There is another silence

Helen What's the job?
John Building a manganese plant. Helping the Third World.
Helen Do you want to help them?
John They seem to be the only people who want to help me. I might as well reciprocate.

Helen is concerned, but irritated by his business with the dustsheet

Helen Do you ever stop for a tea-break?
John Frequently.
Helen Take one now, will you? I'll put the kettle on.
John No. You're the guest. I will.

He goes into the kitchen

Act II, Scene 4

Helen goes to the cupboard and gets out two plates, two cake-forks, and a silver cake-stand. She puts them on the coffee-table and then goes to her plastic bag, and gets out a cake-box. She undoes it, and gently lifts out a large, perfect cheesecake, and puts it on a stand. She puts it on the coffee-table

John comes out of the kitchen, and looks at the cheesecake suspiciously

Bit late for my birthday, isn't it?
Helen It's not a birthday-cake.
John What is it then?
Helen A cheesecake.
John Thanks. But I'm not mad about cheesecake.
Helen It's not an ordinary cheesecake.
John It's a poisoned cheesecake

There is the sound of the granny-flat door opening and closing. Mary comes into the living-room. She walks with the help of a stick, as her ankle is heavily bandaged. Her left arm is in plaster, and is in a sling

Mary (*to Helen*) I thought I heard you.
Helen I was just coming in to see you. How is it today?
Mary The arm's more itchy. So it's getting better. (*Seeing the cheesecake*) That looks nice. What is it?
Helen (*proudly*) A cheesecake.
John You can have my share. I'll make the tea. We can have a family tea-party.

John goes out into the kitchen

Helen Are you all right?
Mary I'm fine. (*Lowering her voice*) Better than that one. (*Gesturing at John, off in kitchen*) Walking bloomin' misery he is. Not that he hasn't been very good to me, but he hasn't smiled for a fortnight.
Helen He feels guilty about you falling like that.
Mary (*more quietly*) That probably isn't all he feels guilty about either.

Helen hears, but ignores this

Helen Look, I'll bring you some tea and cake inside in a minute. I've got to talk to John.
Mary (*alarmed*) Oh dear, you're not going to ...
Helen Mother, I'll tell you all about it when I come in.

Mary, put out at being dismissed, gets up. She hobbles towards the door

Mary (*turning back*) It's none of my business. I don't like to interfere, but you should come back—properly. Otherwise I think he's going to go into the Church.

Mary goes out

John comes back in with a teapot and teacups on a tray

John Where's she gone?

Helen (*businesslike*) I told her I'd come in and see her in a minute. I want to talk to you first.

John sits down and looks at her ominously

John I'm not sure I want to listen. I couldn't concentrate on another problem till about next October. (*He drinks some tea*)
Helen Try the cake.

He looks suspiciously at the cake, and takes a mouthful

I've made a couple of decisions, you should know about. The first's about Val and me.

John reacts violently with a mouthful of cake

John No, please no. I don't want to hear. Do what you like. I'll accept everything—Tom, you, Val. Just get on with it. Just don't tell me. Tell your mother. She'll understand. She listens to those programmes.
Helen Oh, for God's sake, John, don't be so ridiculous. Val and I are separating. Amicably. I'm going to give up my share of the business.
John (*stunned*) What? (*Panicked*) You can't stop working now.
Helen Val and a friend have offered to buy me out. It's a good offer, and suits my plans.

John nibbles at a piece of cake

John What'll you do if you stop working?
Helen I'm not going to stop. I'm going to start up all over again.
John In competition with Val?
Helen No. The deal is I steer clear of pizza. I've had another idea I've done a lot of research on. I thought I'd use the same marketing methods we did with pizza—only for cheesecake. (*Pointing*) That cheesecake. I made it myself.

John eats another small piece

John Um-m. It's quite good.
Helen If you knew anything about cheesecake you'd know that was sensational. I've tried over a dozen recipes. The problem's going to be keeping the quality when it's produced in quantity.
John Um-m.
Helen I'd have to start modestly, of course. Just a few outlets initially. (*Pause*) Now I haven't got Val in tow I thought you might be interested in helping.
John Me?
Helen You.
John I don't know the recipe.
Helen I'll look after the production side. You could help on the business-side.
John Bring all my engineering know-how to the making of cheesecake. Bridges of the stuff, roads ... (*Sarcastically*) I'd be invaluable.
Helen You have to be adaptable these days.

Act II, Scene 4 61

John (*grimly*) Oh, I know that. (*Pause*) And you'd move back in here?
Helen Living together would be more economical, wouldn't it? On the business side we'd draw up a proper legal partnership, of course. That way, if it doesn't work out ...
John Of course, I'll feel terrible about the others.
Helen What others?
John (*gesturing at the cheesecake*) The ones who haven't got a cake. Still, thanks for the offer. I'll think about it.
Helen I'd better go and see Mother. Otherwise she's going to start worrying we're getting divorced. Unless you want to, of course?
John No.

She puts a slice of cake on a plate

Helen Eat up.

Helen takes the plate out, and goes in through her mother's door

John sits with much on his mind. After a moment he takes another slice of cake. He starts to taste it more seriously, like a connoisseur with a vintage wine. The doorbell rings

John gets up and goes out to the front door masticating, thoughtfully

John (*off*) Hello. Come in.

Arthur comes in, followed by John. Arthur has just finished a day's work. He is dressed in corduroy trousers, a check open-necked shirt, and a grubby-looking leather jacket. He looks like a man with a lot on his mind, none of it pleasant

I was having some tea. Want a cup?
Arthur No.

John looks a little apprehensively at him. This isn't jolly old Arthur, or even worried old Arthur. John smiles nervously and gestures at the replastered wall

John Took your advice. I'm putting in a ventilator.

Arthur doesn't look at the wall but keeps his eyes on John

Arthur I don't want to talk about ventilators.
John No. All right.
Arthur I know about you and Gwen.
John What?
Arthur Don't try and play clever with me.
John Know what?
Arthur (*raising his voice*) What you've bloody well been up to with my wife.

John casts an anxious eye towards the hall, worried that Helen will hear

John Please. There's no need to shout.
Arthur Why the hell not?
John (*desperately*) The neighbours.
Arthur I am the neighbours. Gwen's gone.

John Gone?

Arthur Yes. I confronted her with it, and she walked out.

John If she didn't admit it, how do you know?

Arthur You want the squalid details? Right. You knew I was worried about what she was up to, so this morning I checked up on her.

John Checked up?

Arthur Looked in the bedside drawer.

John (*unable to resist*) And she wasn't in there?

Arthur Very funny, aren't we? You should know she's not on the pill. You know where I found her whatsit? In her tracksuit pocket. (*His voice rising*) It doesn't take much imagination to work out who's——

John (*casting a last anxious glance to the hall*) Look, Arthur. I'm sorry ...

Arthur You're what?

John I'm in the middle of trying to think about a job-offer. I'm sorry about——

Arthur (*exploding*) Sorry? You're sorry! You bloody laze around here all day. You've got nothing better to do than ... bloody typical.

John (*responding*) Hang on. Typical? Of what?

Arthur Your bloody sort.

John My sort? You mean the unemployed? You think all over Britain millions of us are fornicating with the wives of men who've gone to work, because it's cheaper than going to the boozer?

Arthur (*shouting back*) You can't hang on to your own miserable wife, so you want mine. Right. You want her, you can have her. You love her, you marry her. I'll divorce her. But *I'm* not supporting you both. Ask Helen if she will.

John (*desperately*) Oh, for Christ's sake, Arthur. I don't want to marry her ... (*Realizing he has gone to far*) Look, I like Gwen ...

Arthur (*staggered*) You fucking like her!

John You've got your adverb in the wrong place.

In a fury Arthur grabs the lapels of John's jacket

Arthur And you've had more than your bloody adverbs in the wrong place.

John (*trying to push Arthur's hands off*) Get off. (*Furiously*) It might be better if you cared more about her.

Arthur (*gripping harder*) What does that mean?

John If you must know, she's too bloody good for you, you bigoted prick.

Arthur And not good enough for you, you idle shit.

He brings his fist up into John's stomach. John gasps. His head goes down on to Arthur's shoulder, and he brings his knee up sharply into Arthur's nether region. Arthur gasps. Both men lurch away from each other, doubled up. They are in front of the coffee-table, heads down, and on a level with the cheesecake on its silver cake-stand. Arthur's gaze lights on the cheesecake

You rotten ...

His hand flashes out and grabs the stem of the cake-stand. His next move is obvious, but John has anticipated it. John grabs Arthur's wrist with both hands

John No, not that.

Act II, Scene 4

Arthur's other hand grasps John's wrist. Both men struggle over the cake, Arthur to throw it, John to prevent him

Helen comes in. She has had a shower and pulled on John's towelling dressing-gown

She stares in amazement at the two men struggling over the cake. They freeze when they see her

Helen What the hell's going on?

John and Arthur let go of each other

John We were fighting over your cake.
Arthur I didn't know you were here.
Helen Ah!
Arthur (*grimly*) I've found out what your husband and my wife are up to.

John sits down, a man prepared to let the storm break over his head

Helen (*coolly*) They jog together.
Arthur That's what you call it. I call it something else.
Helen I know about that too.

John stares at her

Arthur (*shocked*) You've known about it?
Helen Yes.
Arthur For how long?
Helen Does that matter?
Arthur And that's why you left?
Helen No.

Arthur slumps down on the sofa, defeated

Arthur I don't understand. Gwen sleeps with him and comes home to me. You don't bloody care who your husband sleeps with. (*Shaking his head*) I don't understand women any more.
John (*comfortingly to Arthur*) Ah, which of us does?
Arthur I don't want to hear your bloody opinion.
Helen Where is Gwen?
Arthur She walked out this morning. Said she'd got some stupid job to go to.
Helen That's what you've always wanted, isn't it?

The doorbell rings

(*To John*) You'd better go. You'll be safer.

John goes out to the front door

Why don't you have a drink?

Arthur shakes his head miserably, and then jerks up as he hears Gwen's voice

Gwen (*off*) Is Arthur here?

Gwen comes in, followed by John, who is now past reacting to the turn of events. Gwen is dressed as though she has just come from work. She wears a sensible skirt and jumper, and a short, embroidered jacket. She carries a large shoulder bag, modelled on, but not as big as Helen's. In fact she looks strangely similar to Helen in the early part of the play. She looks as though she is going to lash into Arthur, and then spots Helen

Helen Hello, Gwen.
Gwen Oh! Hello, Helen. You're back?
Helen Sort of.
Gwen (*to Arthur*) I saw your car when I got home. I guessed you'd be in here making trouble. (*To John*) I tried to warn you before I went to work but you weren't in.
John Thanks.
Helen (*to Gwen*) Do you want a drink?
Gwen No, thanks.
Helen How's the new job?
Gwen Fine. I'm learning the ropes this week.
Helen Is it full time?
Gwen Yes. I let them talk me into it — when they said they'd throw in the use of a car.
Arthur (*exploding*) I don't believe it. I damn well don't believe it.
Gwen What don't you believe?
Arthur How you two can bloody stand there and talk like that.
Gwen You've had your say from the look of it.
Arthur Yes. I damn well have. They're both barmy. I'm not going on living next to this lot. You can. I'm not.
Gwen Where are you going?
Arthur I don't know, but I'm going. And don't think he wants to live with you either. He doesn't want anything except to draw the dole, and probably have all the other wives in the street too.
Gwen Oh, for God's sake, Arthur. Calm down.
Arthur I won't bloody calm down. If you want to hop round the beds of the unemployed like some sex-starved social-worker, OK. It'll be easier now they're giving you a car.
John Relax, Arthur. Relax.
Arthur Relax. I like that. Is that what you've been doing? (*To Gwen*) I'll tell you one thing. If we stay together, which I very much doubt, it won't be living next to these two. I was brought up to believe you don't ... crap on your own doorstep.

Arthur storms out. There is the sound of the front door banging

Gwen Charming! I'm sorry. He always shouts before he thinks. (*She looks from Helen to John and back*) I'd better go too. Try and calm him down before he has a heart-attack.
Helen Are you going to be all right?
Gwen I'll be fine. If he wants to go he can. (*Awkwardly*) Look, Helen, I'm sorry about ... (*glancing at John*) ... all this.
Helen That's OK. Arthur's the one who doesn't seem to understand.

Act II, Scene 4   65

Gwen Oh, he's furious about everything these days. Business is bad. That's why he's in such a state. He keeps saying he's going to pack it in. Maybe soon he'll be grateful I'm working, if he's not.
Helen Well if he isn't, I won't drop in on him for coffee.
Gwen (*taking the point*) Let's have lunch one day.

Helen nods

'Bye, John.
John 'Bye.

Gwen goes out. Helen goes out with her to the front door

John sits, as one shell-shocked

Helen comes back in, and looks at him

Helen You're very quiet.
John Cat got my tongue.
Helen What happened?
John He insulted the unemployed, and then punched me.
Helen And you thumped him back.
John Had to defend my class. (*Gesturing at the cake*) Anyway I saved the prototype.
Helen Are you all right?
John (*rubbing his middle*) Bit sore, that's all.
Helen I need a drink. (*She goes to the drinks-cabinet*)
John There isn't any. (*Pause. Awkwardly*) I didn't know you knew about—Gwen and me. Is that why you left?
Helen No.
John You didn't care?
Helen Of course I did. What should I have done? Walked out for five reasons instead of four?
John But the business offer is still on?
Helen (*nodding*) Unless, of course, you're desperate to go on jogging—with Gwen.
John No—I think Arthur's put me off a bit.
Helen What about Zambia?
John I've never fancied the climate. Terrible humidity. Anyway I know less about manganese than I do about cheesecake. (*He leans forward and pulls the cheesecake towards him*) I've been thinking about this. How much will they cost to produce?
Helen A lot. I've got all the figures.
John I'd like to see them. Engineers are good at cutting corners.
Helen They still won't be cheap.
John The recession will pass. It will, won't it?
Helen If we live long enough.
John I'm going to live to be a hundred and forty.
Helen If that's your horoscope you read the figures wrong.
John Maybe it said forty and I've survived. (*He picks up the cake-stand with*

the cheesecake on it, and looks at it reverentially) And the Lord spake unto him from out of a cheesecake ...
Helen You've been reading Job again.
John I finished it.
Helen How does he end up?
John With fourteen thousand sheep, six thousand camels, a thousand she-asses ...
Helen Oh, shut up.

He leans over and kisses her. The cake slides off its stand on to the floor, creamy side down

CURTAIN

FURNITURE AND PROPERTY LIST

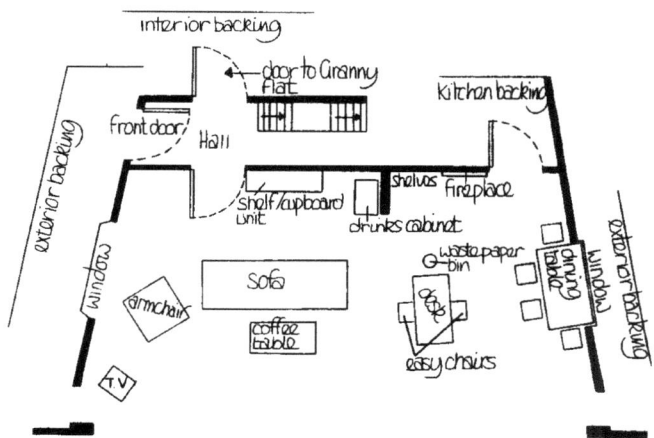

ACT I

Scene 1

On stage: Shelf/cupboard unit. *On shelves:* books (including a Bible with marker set in Book of Job), framed family photographs, copies of professional magazines (including the *Civil Engineer*), files. *Under shelves:* hi-fi set, records, tapes. *In cupboard:* 2 plates, 2 cake forks, silver cake-stand

Victorian glass-fronted cabinet. *In it:* glasses, bottle of sherry, empty bottle of whisky, full bottle of malt whisky, almost empty bottle of brandy

Victorian fireplace

Sofa. *On it:* cushions

Coffee-table

Armchair

2 easy chairs

Desk. *On it:* phone, phone directory, phone book, note-pad. *By it:* wastepaper-basket

Dining-table

4 chairs

Wall mirror

Curtains at windows open

Off stage: Briefcase containing files and papers, executive diary **(John)**
Ice for drink **(John)**
Large sling shoulder bag containing files, papers etc. **(Helen)**
Dish of nuts **(Helen)**
Onion, margarine, pizza wrapped in clingfilm **(Mary)**

Personal: **John:** wristwatch (worn throughout)
Mary: wristwatch (worn throughout)
Helen: wristwatch (worn throughout)
Arthur: wristwatch (worn throughout)
Gwen: wristwatch (worn throughout)

Scene 2

Strike: Used glasses, dish of nuts

Set: Newspapers, journals, copy of the *Civil Engineer* on sofa
Large map of Greater London pasted to a board with small red and blue squares stuck on it, various graphs, charts, etc., pens, sheaf of c.v.s, papers on desk
Curtains open

Offstage: Small shopping bag containing half a dozen eggs, butter, washing powder **(Gwen)**

Scene 3

Strike: Newspapers, journals etc. from sofa

Set: Pocket calculator, papers, blue folder containing papers, **Helen**'s sling shoulder bag on dining-table
Living-room door open

Off stage: Dirty towels **(Helen)**
Postcard, several letters including official brown envelope containing dole cheque **(John)**
Carpet-sweeper, duster **(John)**
Large shopping basket containing purse **(Gwen)**
2 mugs of coffee **(John)**
Large sling shoulder bag **(Helen)**

Scene 4

Strike: Large shopping basket
2 mugs of coffee
Hoover
Postcard, letters

Set: New bottle of whisky for **Helen**
Helen's evening-coat on chair

Off stage: Bottle of milk **(Mary)**
Burned out saucepan **(Helen)**
Electric guitar-case, duffel-bag **(Tom)**
Electronic guitar unit **(Tom)**
Glass of orange juice **(Tom)**

Personal: **Tom:** chunky silver chain, 1 ear-ring
John: black bow-tie in pocket
Arthur: black bow-tie in pocket

ACT II

Scene 1

Strike: Used glass
Victorian fireplace from dining area revealing gaping hole

Re-set: Bible on shelf
Desk and easy chair in living-room area

Set: Dust sheet and small pile of rubble in front of gaping hole
Dust sheets over sofa and chairs
Hoover by kitchen door
Brush and bucket for **John**

Off stage: Guitar-case, small suitcase (**Tom**)
Glass of orange juice (**Tom**)
2 mugs of coffee (**Gwen**)

Personal: **Tom:** gold chain round neck

Scene 2

Strike: All dust sheets
Used mugs and glass
Hoover

Off stage: Glass of orange juice (**John**)
Large brass candlestick (**Mary**)
Floorcloth (**Tom**)

Personal: **Gwen:** handbag
Tom: tin containing reefer

Scene 3

On stage: As previous scene

Off stage: Tray containing glass of orange juice, bowl of cereal, jug of milk, spoon (**Mary**)
Tray containing plate of toast, butter, knife, mug of coffee (**Mary**)
2 mugs of coffee (**Gwen**)

Scene 4

Strike: Used mugs, glasses, plates, cutlery, butter etc.

Re-set: Desk and easy chair as in Act I

Set: Plaster with ventilator gap covering fireplace hole
Dust sheet in front of plastered-up fireplace
Broom

Off stage: Large sling shoulder bag, plastic shopping bag containing cheesecake in a
 box **(Helen)**
 Plaster and trowel **(John)**
 Tray containing teapot, 2 cups and saucers, jug of milk **(John)**
 Large sling shoulder bag **(Gwen)**

Personal: **Mary:** Walking stick, plaster cast, arm-sling, ankle-bandage

LIGHTING PLOT

Practical fittings required: 3 table lamps, pendant light, TV

Interior. The same scene throughout

ACT I SCENE 1. Early evening

To open: Late sunshine effect

Cue 1	**Mary** switches on the television *Snap on TV effect*	(Page 3)
Cue 2	**Helen** turns off the television *Snap off TV effect*	(Page 3)
Cue 3	**Helen** draws the curtains *Reduce lighting*	(Page 12)
Cue 4	**Mary** goes out into the kitchen *Black-out. When ready bring up interior light in hall*	(Page 12)
Cue 5	**Helen** switches on main light in living-room *Snap on pendant light and general interior lighting*	(Page 12)
Cue 6	**John** puts the phone down, a contented smile on his face *Black-out*	(Page 15)

ACT I SCENE 2. Morning

To open: Bright sunshine effect

Cue 7	**John** touches the wood on the desk twice and goes out *Black-out*	(Page 19)

ACT I SCENE 3. Morning

To open: Bright sunshine effect

Cue 8	**Gwen** and **John** go out and upstairs. Pause *Slight lighting change*	(Page 26)
Cue 9	**Mary** goes back into her flat *Fade to Black-out*	(Page 27)

ACT I SCENE 4. Early evening

To open: Late sunshine effect

No cues

ACT II SCENE 1. Morning

To open: Bright sunshine effect

Cue 10	**Helen** goes out and slams the door *Black-out*	(Page 45)

ACT II SCENE 2. Night

To open: Dim night light effect through window

Cue 11	**John** switches on living-room lights *Snap on pendant light and table lamp with bright interior lighting and covering spot*	(Page 45)
Cue 12	**John** turns off main light *Reduce overall lighting, snap off pendant*	(Page 45)
Cue 13	**John** puts on second table lamp *Snap on table lamp and covering spot*	(Page 45)
Cue 14	**John** turns on another lamp *Snap on covering spot and increase lighting*	(Page 45)
Cue 15	**John** switches off the lights *Snap off interior effect and covering spots in sequence, leaving dim night light effect through window*	(Page 46)
Cue 16	Sound of fridge door opening *Snap on fridge light effect in kitchen area*	(Page 47)
Cue 17	Fridge is shut *Snap off fridge light*	(Page 47)
Cue 18	**Gwen** switches on living-room light *Snap on pendant light and bring up overall interior effect*	(Page 47)
Cue 19	**John:** "Oh God!" *Fade to Black-out*	(Page 50)

ACT II SCENE 3. Morning

To open: Bright sunshine effect

Cue 20	**Arthur:** "Seventeen, Forsythe Road ..." *Fade to Black-out*	(Page 57)

ACT II SCENE 4. Morning

To open: Bright sunshine effect

No cues

EFFECTS PLOT

Please read the notice on page vi concerning the use of copyright material.

ACT I

Cue 1	**John** goes back into the kitchen *Sound of fridge door opening and ice-trays being rattled, then sound of fridge door closing*	(Page 2)
Cue 2	**Mary** switches on the television *Bring up TV sound to normal level*	(Page 3)
Cue 3	**Mary** turns up the television volume *Increase TV volume*	(Page 3)
Cue 4	**Helen** turns off the television *Snap off TV sound*	(Page 3)
Cue 5	**John:** "I told you Coleman cancelled the lunch ..." *Doorbell*	(Page 5)
Cue 6	**Helen:** "... while I tidy myself up." *Double knock on front door*	(Page 5)
Cue 7	**Helen:** "... the time to get round to it." *Phone*	(Page 10)
Cue 8	**Mary:** "Oh!" *Car hooting impatiently*	(Page 12)
Cue 9	**John** crosses to the sofa and back to the desk *Doorbell*	(Page 15)
Cue 10	**Mary:** "... about gas and electricity charges ..." *Phone*	(Page 17)
Cue 11	**Helen** does some sums on her pocket calculator *Phone*	(Page 19)
Cue 12	**John** screws his face up *Doorbell*	(Page 22)
Cue 13	**John:** "You never stand still for long enough." *Muted sound of car drawing up, followed by car horn*	(Page 34)

ACT II

Cue 14	**Tom** goes towards the living-room door *Phone*	(Page 38)
Cue 15	**John** switches on the Hoover *Vacuum with crackling effect, sputtering into silence as in text*	(Page 41)

Cue 16	**Tom** goes into the kitchen *Sound of fridge door opening, glass clinking, something being poured and put back in fridge and fridge door closing*	(Page 47)
Cue 17	**Mary** goes into the kitchen *Sound of china rattling etc. from kitchen*	(Page 51)
Cue 18	**John:** "So do I." *Doorbell*	(Page 53)
Cue 19	**Gwen:** "Did you sleep at all last night?" *Phone*	(Page 54)
Cue 20	**Gwen:** "... to go on eating out." *Doorbell*	(Page 55)
Cue 21	**John:** "Terrific." *Thump from hall direction*	(Page 57)
Cue 22	**Arthur:** "Seventeen, Forsythe Road ..." *Sound of ambulance siren swelling*	(Page 57)
Cue 23	**John** starts to taste the cake more seriously *Doorbell*	(Page 61)
Cue 24	**Helen:** "That's what you've always wanted, isn't it?" *Doorbell*	(Page 63)

MUSIC PLOT

A license issued by Samuel French Ltd to perform this play does not include permission to use the Overture and Incidental music specified in this copy. Where the place of performance is already licensed by the Performing Right Society a return of the music used must be made to them. If the place of performance is not so licensed then application should be made to the PERFORMING RIGHT SOCIETY, 29 Berners Street, London W1.

A separate and additional licence from PHONOGRAPHIC PERFORMANCES LTD, Ganton House, Ganton Street, London W1, is needed whenever commercial recordings are used.

Cue 1	Before the CURTAIN rises *Errol Garner recording of "Summertime". Fade when ready*	(Page 1)
Cue 2	To open SCENE 2 *Oscar Peterson recording of "On A Clear Day"*	(Page 15)
Cue 3	**John** turns off the hi-fi *Cut music*	(Page 15)
Cue 4	Black-out *Joe Pass recording of "Nice Work If You Can Get It"*	(Page 19)
Cue 5	**John** switches on the hi-fi *Errol Garner recording of "Dreamy"*	(Page 21)
Cue 6	**John** turns the volume down slightly *Reduce volume slightly*	(Page 22)
Cue 7	**John** turns the tape off *Cut music*	(Page 22)
Cue 8	**John** puts a record on *Art Tatum recording of "Somebody Loves Me"*	(Page 30)
Cue 9	**Helen** turns the hi-fi off *Cut music*	(Page 30)
Cue 10	**John** puts on a record *Oscar Peterson recording of "You Stepped Out Of A Dream"*	(Page 34)
Cue 11	**John** turns the hi-fi down *Reduce volume*	(Page 35)
Cue 12	**John** turns the hi-fi up *Increases volume*	(Page 35)

Cue 13	**John** turns the hi-fi down *Cut music*	(Page 35)
Cue 14	**John** turns up the sound on the hi-fi *Oscar Peterson recording of "Watch What Happens". Fade when ready*	(Page 36)

ACT II

Cue 15	Black-out *J. J. Johnson recording of "What Is This Thing Called Love". Fade when ready*	(Page 45)
Cue 16	As ambulance siren swells *Fade in J. J. Johnson and Stan Getz recording of "My Funny Valentine". Fade when ready*	(Page 57)

WHY ME?

Seen at London's Strand Theatre in 1985, Stanley Price's trenchant, very funny comedy about unemployment starred Richard Briers as the redundant civil engineer battling against the odds to find a job.

"... Mr Price has come up with a bright, alert, deftly observant play. Without beating drums or waving banners, he makes the point that in these sour times joblessness saps social confidence; and, more positively, that men and women must behave as equal partners rather than breadwinners and dependents ... good comedy (like this) is tethered to the real world." *The Guardian*

"Stanley Price has suceeded in treating a serious subject with incisive wit and much pathos." *Time Out*

"An important event in British theatre ... It's something halfway between a realistic farce and a situation-tragedy" *The Sunday Times*

John Bailey returns to his South London home a member of the "over three million club" and bitter recipient of a "tarnished chrome" handshake. In the course of the ensuing summer he struggles bravely with job rejections; loss of dignity in the face of his wife Helen's hugely successful pizza business; an adulterous affair with the next door neighbour; the incipient break up of his marriage; the shattering revelation that his teenage son is a transvestite rock musician; and repeated forays into his living-room by his mother-in-law who refuses to stay in her adjoining granny-flat. He finds comfort in the Book of Job, seeing it as a parable for the recession and, eventually, like his biblical counterpart, the ending is a happy one. He is united with Helen, both in marriage, once again, and in a rather tasty new business venture!

ISBN 0-573-01622-4

9 780573 016226

www.ingramcontent.com/pod-product-compliance
Ingram Content Group UK Ltd.
Pitfield, Milton Keynes, MK11 3LW, UK
UKHW021840210426
5322IPUK00022B/388